My Father's House

Mathew Daniel

Published by Mathew Daniel, 2024.

While every precaution has been taken in the preparation of this book, the publisher assumes no responsibility for errors or omissions, or for damages resulting from the use of the information contained herein.

MY FATHER'S HOUSE

First edition. November 1, 2024.

Copyright © 2024 Mathew Daniel.

ISBN: 979-8227996053

Written by Mathew Daniel.

Table of Contents

A Tribute . . . Long Overdue

To my parents, Rachel and Daniel, who, through their selflessness in helping others worse off than us, giving when they had so little to give, taught me life lessons and the true meaning of purpose, love, and mindfulness. They left the world a better place.

My Father's House
by
Mathew Daniel

Stepping Back in Time

Memories from seven decades ago—my childhood—borne of joy, challenge, and wonder—were threadbare like a well-worn tapestry. With a weaver's determination, I revived some of their faded hues and lost luminescence through photographs, old and new, and conversations with those in the know during visits to India as recently as 2023. To safeguard privacy, I altered names and details. To sharpen the narrative, I reshaped and reimagined certain scenes in the final chapters to bring out aspects of our shared humanity while maintaining the essence of those formative years.

Now, in my seventies, as I trace the seventeen-year arc the book is about—from the innocence of Montessori to my tumultuous adolescence—I invite you to step back with me on that journey, that my parents prepared me for. They faced our circumstances with fortitude, thus awakening me and helping me face that world. My book, dedicated to my parents, is a long-overdue tribute.

This is a heartfelt story, a child's viewpoint. If it lingers, resonates—please share your thoughts on the bookseller's website.

Prologue: Death Sentence

Imagine Bombay during the monsoon season: a force field of never-ending rain interrupted by intense heat. In this regard, 1965 saw unprecedented rainfall—a record-breaking year. Between spells of torrential rain, the sultriness resumed where it had left off in late May. The insane heat and mugginess could knock you out if the deluge did not drown you. It was not an ideal time for traveling. During the mid-morning hours on a Saturday in July of that year, my father and I arrived at the free government hospital and headed to the doctor's office. I did not look forward to these visits because the ebullient bedside manner of the doctor, whom I shall call Dr. Joshi, took an about-turn after Dad informed him he could not afford his private clinic. Unbeknownst to me, this would also be our last visit.

The doctor, splendidly attired, approached the doorway. He was short and stocky with a button nose. The hair, wavy and unnaturally black for a man in his early 60s, was combed straight back in an attempt, I suppose, to cover the large bald spot on his head. He compensated for his nondescript presence with an overarching show of sartorial elegance: a navy-blue bow tie, off-white sharkskin trousers, and jacket. The winged insets of his patent-leather oxfords had fresh chalk. He looked like a pukka sahib, ready to hightail it to the Bombay Race Course or somewhere fine for the Saturday afternoon and hobnob with the elite. His smock, dispatched in a hurry, dangled in disarray on the hanger.

Dad, conversely, could not afford, nor would he consider, such stylish overreach. As a younger man, he dressed nicely for work, cutting a dapper figure with his cuff links and Tootal brand tie to complement his jacket, long-sleeved shirt, and trousers. However, he always wore clothes made of swadeshi, domestically produced cotton, even after the accident, when he switched to off-white bush shirts and white trousers and discarded the rest. This morning, Dad wore his flimsy black rubber rain shoes since his only pair of leather shoes had been 'cobblered' to oblivion, succumbing before the monsoons could drown them. The rain shoes had long lost their shininess because he had worn them since the start of the monsoons in late May. The sparseness of the hair on his head, which he combed back without any parting, and his well-rounded paunch, much like the worn-out rubber rain shoes, did not bother him. People who knew him and knew of him held him in high esteem. He was friends with public figures. Even as a child, though Dad's luminaries to our one-room tenement cut on my time with him, I sensed something bigger than me was afoot. He had spoken at political rallies during the heady days of India's struggle for freedom from the British. He had been a vital member of the Government of Bombay Consumers' Advisory Committee during and after World War II. Many still looked up to him and sought his counsel. He had a presence marked by a quick, short gait, equally quick wit, and bright, deep-set brown eyes behind metal-rimmed glasses.

I was fortunate I had someone like him to look up to. He made up for his professorial frumpiness by engaging effortlessly with his keen intellect, helpful nature, humor, and sincerity. He was someone whose curiosity knew no bounds, who, besides as a member of J. N. Petit Library, which was over a hundred years old, devoured everything from domestic and international newspapers to Toynbee, Gibbon, Macaulay, Russell, Gandhi, Nehru... you name it.

When illness struck him, my once vibrant Dad, his gait slowed, and his eyes dimmed neither turned a page nor cracked a smile or a joke. How sad it was to watch him, and I so yearned to see him well as we rushed to the doctor's office on the top floor.

Dad's perspiration lit up his face and balding head. His sparse hair and clothes looked disheveled.

After assisting him during our two-hour journey, which should usually have taken half that time from Wadala, a Bombay suburb where we lived, I was tired, too. I could well imagine how exhausted he was, given his condition.

The weakness and pain in his legs had worsened, and episodes of imbalance and temporary disorientation had become alarmingly frequent. Dr. Joshi, neurology head at the hospital, had visiting hours on Thursday afternoons and Saturday mornings. Instead of the free consultation on that fateful Saturday, my father got much more than he bargained for.

"You are late," the doctor admonished, tapping his oversized gold watch several times with his index finger. His normally protuberant eyes stuck out even further, and the heavy gray bags under them puffed up even more.

"What do you people think? Is this a railway station where you can come and go as you please?" he said, herding us to the examination table. The Indian Railways was a euphemism for everything wrong with the country since it touched every facet of life as India's largest employer.

"Mrs. Gupte put him down for next week. I am getting late already," he said while Mrs. Gupte pulled a tattered screen around us. The doctor did not care to wear his smock as he did a quick once-over of Dad without a word. The no-touch examination took less than a minute.

"Mrs. Gupte, he should come next week," he repeated, addressing Dad in the third person. He then abruptly steered towards the corridor and raced to the elevators after having met the custom of seeing every scheduled patient. Not even the plight of the disabled, helpless figure next to me would change his mind.

"Next week? Doctor sahib, this pain is unbearable. I need some relief from this—samples—anything. I know we are late after traveling long to get here," my father cried out at the departing figure.

"Please. Doctor... please"

The man was not going to turn around. He was not about to return for a thorough examination of Dad and give the needed medicine. Hardly able to walk, my father leaned heavily on me as we shuffled in pursuit. I do not know what made my father pursue the striding figure. It was sheer desperation or a classic demonstration of his undying optimism. He held on to me with his only arm—his right arm. When I was nine, a devastating car accident severed his left arm at the scene, turning our world inside out. Finally, Dad stopped, unable to carry on. The doctor paused and turned around, realizing the only footsteps he heard were his own. It took him a few seconds to come up with the words I least expected from a doctor, a healer.

"You—your case is hopeless," he yelled. He cast his exophthalmic gaze toward me and lanced me with a piercing look.

The empty corridor reverberated with his decree. Stunned, Dad involuntarily smacked his forehead with his only hand as I, with both arms, prevented him from losing balance.

The statement hung like a guillotine for the longest time before Damocles brought down the sword on Dad. It was a death sentence. The light in his bright eyes flickered. What I saw before they closed for a few moments was the glazed eyes of a fish in its final throes. I think that's when he lost his will to live. First, it was the accident, and then this. They say tragedies come in threes. A stampede followed.

PROLOGUE PICTURE: Sitting: Dad is second from left.

Before, during, and after WWII, ration cards became an unpleasant reality for staple food items like rice and wheat. Dad was one of 13 members on the government-appointed advisory committee.

Chapter 1: Becoming a Story Teller

The doctor could not break Dad's unwavering spirit, and I could see Dad was readying himself to disprove the doctor's dire prognosis. His stricken eyes brightened somewhat as they turned towards me. He told me to keep the incident from Ma. At a loss for words, I nodded in agreement. Those moments have sustained me ever since. His indomitable inner strength and insight, storied in the community, were his trademarks. Eight years earlier, with quick thinking and daring, he slammed the door on the grim reaper following a motorcar accident near a fishing village northwest of Bombay that all but killed him.

However, this time, the enemy was different, invisible. Dad was battling a bacterial invasion that remained misdiagnosed, misunderstood, and mistreated. Following the death sentence at the doctor's office, the pain worsened, Dad stopped working, and I stayed home to help. With his usual confidence, he promised his visitors, mainly his worried office mates who lived in the same railway quarters as us, that he would be back soon, even heartier. Regrettably, he fainted a few weeks later on a rainy Sunday afternoon. I rushed into the downpour to get the railway dispensary doctor, who told us to take him to the hospital. We rushed to the hospital in a taxi, with me in the passenger seat, counting the minutes and Ma comforting Dad in the back.

I hoped we would not come across my nemesis. However, the doctor was there doing rounds on a Sunday and acknowledged us with a sour face. A few weeks later, he did experimental brain surgery on Dad, after which Dad never opened his eyes. During those coma-riddled days, I gabbed to Dad, hoping he would wake up so I could say a proper goodbye. Those eyes and ears, though, remained shut.

Only years later did I realize the doctor's words, uttered with such deft detachment, came from his profession's rarified position and entitled social status. Sitting by Dad, I wished I had jotted down the thoughts drowning me. I was determined to write about it all one day, although I was no writer like my brother John. Ten years older than me, he had already published a few short stories in the Times of India. During Dad's final months, my thoughts of writing about my experience had a fatal circularity when my brother, with his smart-alecky tin ear, brought home a novel with an ominous, unnerving title —A Death in the Family by James Agee. It took a few years after Dad's passing before he would admit his obtuseness.

When Dad, the linchpin that held us together, left us, bereavement fell by the wayside as India's age-old social underbelly, simmering in the background at home during Dad's last months, boiled over, resulting in an unimagined plot twist. There was more material to sift, even as the heat of the stampede took its toll, and my procrastination got the better of me, as my book idea lay dormant. I wrote a few words here and there about Dad, but nothing substantive. My brother scoffed at a short story I wrote called 'Next Time Man' about an indecisive character who put off doing anything and everything. Then, engineering studies in India preceded three voyages on the high seas as a Junior Engineering Officer in the British Merchant Navy, which provided enough for enrolling in graduate engineering studies. Mainly because of cost, and some other considerations I chose the University of Oklahoma in the US over Cranfield University, a post-grad institution in pretty Bedfordshire, UK.

In 1995, the Oklahoma City terrorist bombing affected a friend, and I weaved a novella around the incident. Still, nary a line about life with Dad passed from me to the head of a pen. Picasso said there is nothing more difficult than a line, which I think was my predicament. However, I know he was not talking about writing.

Finally, fate nudged me with a subdural hematoma in 2010, which landed me in Intensive Care for three days out of town in Philadelphia. The hematoma awakened me to my fragility, shook my laissez-faire perspective, and magnified my life experiences front and center. I suspect that, unknowingly, I was reaching a turning point. A month and a half later, somewhat recovered, I returned to work, not registering it as a wake-up call. A small course change, a few years later, took me to ten-day silent meditation courses annually at an out-of-state center for the next five years, until 2019, and in 2017 to a monastery for a week during a three-week trip to Thailand.

Meanwhile, on my way home from work, another nudge came on a Thursday evening in 2014. This time, an accident on I-35 during busy office hours totaled my car. Involuntarily hitting the brakes saved me as I sped towards the suddenly stationary large truck I was following. The truck's bumper loomed large as I frantically pumped the brakes. My mangled hood crumpled and screeched to rest within inches of my windshield as the truck's bumper shaved off my engine. I was too stunned to feel fear and did not see flashes of my greatest hits rushing by. I only knew I was unbelievably fortunate.

The next day, slumped in bed, aching all over, memories came of another person dear to me in another accident at another time. The urgency of the second nudge, the accident signified, edged me into early retirement that year so I could keep my promise to a comatose man as he lay dying. My accident was the spark. Those free lifelines given to me had Dad written all over them, bringing clarity and resolution.

Retiring early was about settling unfinished business: telling my story. Those 17 event-filled years with Dad, Ma, and others, initially entitled 'In My Father's House,' live in me. Transitioning into full-time writing, an ascetic, immersive, and mostly inward-looking profession required a significant shift, including within the immediate family, where I had happily contributed more than my fair share until my early retirement. I refused to play houseboy, at least not to the extent I used to. Bringing justice to the task meant raking those emotional embers, reflecting and focusing my energies, recreating from that curious boy's well-remembered and not-so-well-remembered recollections, in solitude within those walls, unencumbered. In so doing, I discovered the boy's voice in its telling.

———◉———

I GREW UP WATCHING my parents in action, two saints in my view, as they took on the arduous task of helping those who were worse off, despite our own fraught and miserable circumstances. My siblings, John and Elisabeth, understood its mechanics better than I did since, being much younger than the two, I was oblivious to how my parents' selflessness affected all our lives. My parents' world-saving mission had an address—24, Sabita Building, Dadar—our one-room tenement in Bombay's mill town district.

My parents, Rachel Thomas and E. K. Daniel, were born in 1917 and 1913, respectively, in the princely states of Travancore & Cochin on the west coast of South India. Most people from Travancore, called Malayalis, spoke Malayalam, one of South India's Dravidian languages. Travancore, drenched in history, is over a thousand miles south of Bombay. From ancient times (the spice route circa 3000 BCE), it was world-renowned for its spices and attracted traders from the Middle East and beyond. Tradition holds that St. Thomas, the doubting apostle, visited Travancore around 52 CE. Christianity there goes back to around that time.

Dad (Achachan in Malayalam) was born in Mylapra, a village in Travancore, into a Brethren family, an extreme fringe Christian group. The 'E' stands for Elempilakal, Dad's house name. He was the youngest and shortest of eight children, and his middle initial K is Kochu (little one or shorty) in Malayalam. His mother died during his birth. His oldest brother's wife played Cruella and mistreated him until he was 11. His brothers never did much schooling and worked the pitiful land that remained after Grandpa had squandered most of it in shady deals. Dad escaped to Kozhencherry, 10 miles away, where the nearest high school happened to be. He lived there with a family that belonged to the town's leading Christian community, a comparatively progressive denomination called the Mar Thoma Orthodox Syrian Christians (Marthomites for short), established in 1599. 'Syrian' denotes the Syriac tradition and liturgy they still follow. Unlike the Brethren, Daniel's reform-minded surrogate family loved him like their own children. The sensitive lad changed significantly.

In the late 1920s, 15-year-old Daniel, Mylapra's first matriculate, fluent in English and Malayalam, left the grinding poverty for his first job in Madras (Chennai since 1996), on India's southeast coast.

He was the well-versed, multilingual *babu* (clerk) the British Raj needed. He became a senior claims department clerk at Bombay Port Trust (BPT) Railways. Bombay (Mumbai since 1995) was the state capital of Bombay State, which in 1960 separated into Gujarat and Maharashtra states. Known as Maharashtrians, the locals spoke Marathi.

Even though he was at odds with his Brethren relatives and childhood friends regarding how they behaved and practiced Christianity, he did not forget them. Beginning with Madras, he helped their matriculated children. The matriculates stayed with him in Madras until he found them jobs. After he moved to Bombay, married Ma, and had three children, he kept the commitment rigorously. Rachel was always his eager collaborator.

Ma (*Amachi*), a Marthomite, was born in Kozhencherry. Rachel was the youngest in her family, which consisted of a boy and three girls. Daniel's best friend was Rachel's older brother. He knew the siblings well since they went to the same school. I heard he had an eye on Rachel from early on. Rachel and her older sister dropped out of school because it became unaffordable to her widowed mother. Soon after, at 12, restless Rachel decided to go to Madurai, a town in neighboring Madras, for assistant nurse training at Erskine Hospital (now Rajaji Hospital). As a result, Ma was fluent in Tamil, the Dravidian language spoken in Madras, and received a healthy dose of Carnatic music, various dance forms, and stories from Hindu mythology by regularly visiting the nearby Meenakshi Temple across the Vaigai River. She was homesick throughout her time there and fell ill a few months before completing training. Her brother brought her back home. Her nursing training came in handy all throughout her life. In addition to her fluency in Tamil and Malayalam, she also had a smattering of English.

Daniel broke Brethren tradition and married Rachel in the Kochu Palli (small church) of the Marthomites in the mid-1930s, then moved to Bombay. Next to the Velya Palli (big church), constructed in 1941, the small church still stands as a testament to the humble origins of the reformist group after the split.

In Ma, Dad found someone as intent on helping others as he was. Their mission was to help beyond their own and their children's privation. These mostly matriculated youngsters stayed with us until Dad found them jobs in Bombay, other cities in India, or the Middle East. He borrowed to keep this going since he did not make enough for his own family to get by, let alone two or three job seekers at a time. By the time of his accident, when he was 44, nearly a hundred kids from almost as many families had lived in our tenement for varying periods. Dad helped many more than the ones who stayed with us. Simply put, the multiplier effect of their philanthropy on the families and subsequent generations they helped was gigantic.

Pioneers like Dad helped in making modern Kerala. In helping others, Dad tested Ma's stamina in every possible way. While they continued their thankless mission, the two doted on us and instilled a civic sense and a lifelong love for reading, the arts, and science. In this confined living space, I constantly clashed with my siblings, John and Elisabeth, ten and six years older than me. I was born at the free Wadia Maternity Hospital in the adjacent mill town of Parel, where I received the best care I could get in a public hospital. I was under the watchful eye of Ma's best friend, Matron Mary, the matron of all nurses at Wadia, who became my godmother. It was not as if anyone else was waiting for that lifetime appointment.

My siblings enjoyed grandma's care for a long while after their births in the luxury of the Kerala countryside before Ma returned to Bombay. Their early 'sitting up' pictures show well-fed, chubby babies. Ma decided it was best to have me in Bombay and not disrupt my siblings' schooling.

Many Bombay schools, with Marathi, English, and other languages as the medium of instruction, charged a small fee. The Maharashtra government built free primary Marathi Municipal schools for the locals to encourage local education. Since instruction for college and studies beyond high school was in English, we went to English-medium schools.

John constantly called me a *potten* (idiot), and so did Elisabeth, who also called me *bhaiya* (milkman). Though bhaiya was an endearing term for 'brother' in the Hindi-speaking states of India, it meant 'milkman' in Bombay. Young men from these states sported a ridiculous tuft of hair or *shendi* several inches long that stuck out behind their heads, came in droves to Bombay, and mainly sold milk. There was no mistaking what Elisabeth meant by bhaiya. They could have called me worse names, though I most resented 'idiot.' Such monikers stick around, and you become them. I realized too late that there are no such things as nice bullies, only perfect ones.

Being much younger, I was an open book to them, as predictable as a tortoise.

It was fun when they played with me on rare occasions. Elisabeth and I invented a language called '*Gurgu*,' with crucial English and Malayalam words spelled backward. We tripped up on our invention many times before getting it somewhat right. Sometimes, John would let me thumb through his stamp collection. My curiosity was insatiable as I looked at those pages. Once I started to read, I learned the names of countries spelled on their stamps. Magyar for Hungary, Éire for Ireland, and Siam for Thailand are a few I recall. Then there was his red, cloth-bound, dog-eared Pears' Cyclopaedia that held secrets about everything. Before I lost myself in its pages in utter wonderment, I'd steal a peek or two at the picture on the inside cover: a pretty little girl in full color, about to blow soap bubbles from a bowl, and I wondered why she was so pensive and sad. Often, he let me install the stylus, wind the gramophone, and play his 78s. However, he had to endure the faux jollity of 'Buttons and Bows' every time before I played his requests—Frank Sinatra's (Tender Trap, All the Way) and Cole Porter's (When They Begin the Beguine). Aunt Saramma (Sara for short) brought me 'Buttons and Bows' after one of her many foreign trips, and it's still one of my all-time favorites.

Once, Sara brought us two cans of cheese that had wind-up openers. I remember those yellow cans because of the tiger's headshot on them. The next day, we went for a picnic at Bassein Fort. Amidst the ruins of the old fort, John ceremoniously opened the cheese cans, and we had it with tea made over a fire. I tasted cheese for the first time, which they said was nothing like paneer, a north Indian cheese, and this was news to me since I had never tasted paneer either. Before my birth, Sara and her brother, George, lived with us while job-hunting. Although unrelated to us, we called them Uncle and Aunt because they were Dad's contemporaries.

Most of the bullying I endured at home did not affect me because I always forgave them. All I wanted was their acceptance. Ma admired my ability to forgive and forget; she was only half-right, since she only got the forgiving part right. As much as I tried, I could not forget.

John was the favorite—the firstborn boy in a patriarchal South Indian Malayali household. He captured everyone's attention, along with the food, premium bed space in a not-so-premium environment, the clothes, and everything else. My brother grew up to be six feet tall, a feat unheard of in a land where the average height for men was five feet two inches during those early years after independence. He was the best built in the family, including our uncles and cousins. He made a big show of crunching two sheets of the Times of India with one hand. At the same time, he lifted our wooden chair by one of its legs with the other as if it were nothing, imitating his mentor, Charles Atlas, the famous American bodybuilder. With money he had pestered from Dad, he even bought records for the gramophone. He had nice clothes, especially after high school. I still remember his trousers tailored from gabardine, a twill worsted wool fabric, imported, of course, and the fine rayon shirt he wore when he went off to college—this in a land with the cheapest and best cotton and silk! To me, he would always remain the suave and smooth Mr. Gabardine. In short, he thought of himself as the complete package until I got old enough to shred that theory.

My brother had four years of one-on-one attention before Elisabeth showed up. The Bombay Malayali crowd gurgled at the pretty thing—all fair, chubby, and bouncy with light eyes and a mop of black hair. Elisabeth had a pleasant smile and the cherubic, dimpled cheeks of an angel. She got the rock star treatment, too. She grew up as tall as Dad at five feet four inches, unheard of for a girl in our community. I remember her silky white skirt, custom-made from the finest thread, because I accidentally ruined it with the hot iron. She shunned me for days, even though Ma expertly repaired it. I also knew gabardine since I ironed my brother's clothes, too.

I arrived at the tail end, demanding my share of love and scarce resources. I was fearless among the Daniels and was hell-bent on getting attention. Ma took care of me from the start. Ma said she ate plenty of the amply available *payyer* (mung beans), which gave her much-needed protein when she carried me. Dad could ill-afford other protein sources such as eggs and meat; for some reason, I grew up loving anything with mung beans. They adoringly called me the *payer-kunj,* or the child who loved mung beans. The food rationing was at its meanest for basic staples like rice and wheat during the post-WWII and post-Independence periods. When I first started 'wobbling' on my tummy, my picture shows a somewhat scrawny nematode, all head and nothing much else, different from the chubby, farm-fed tykes I mentioned earlier.

According to Ma and others, being the littlest, whatever I said came out funny. I tried making sense of the world I faced daily, often wondering aloud instinctively. More importantly, I saw my world as it was—comical and clumsy, full of love and fellowship, at times uplifting and depressing, replete with hunger and despair. It was always uncaring and unforgiving, with little triumphs sparingly sprinkled here and there, so I did not entirely lose hope.

My imagination ran rampant as I looked out our window at the activities on the street. I was bug-eyed from watching people marching up and down our street from my third-floor vantage. I often imitated them in front of my family, especially Ma, who would bend backward with laughter. I was the family court jester—even more reason my siblings took me for a nitwit, someone they could trample with impunity.

Early one morning, while kneeling on a chair at the window, looking out mainly at the empty street below, and daydreaming,

I overheard Elisabeth talking to John about me in our makeshift bedroom.

"Will I have to stop calling him an idiot, too? They will never send him to Thana." Bombay's only asylum was in a suburb called Thana.

"We can always call him something else," my brother chortled.

Good, my brother was coming to his senses. I was sure Ma persuaded him to stop teasing me, and, in turn, he was trying to convince Elisabeth. I would not mind them calling me a milkman if it finally meant that I was no longer an idiot. Their conversation was long and unintelligible, and they both laughed at its tail end. It sounded like they had something up their sleeves. As I listened to them, my face reddened at some of the indignities I had endured serving time as the youngest.

The two hurried next to me, and we silently watched the world. Why couldn't we always be like this, a perfect threesome, watching life unfold below on Main Road, as the rising sun filtered through the fronds of the coconut trees behind the Muslim restaurant, casting a surreal reddish hue on our handsome faces?

I reminded myself to curb my imagination and be wary of them. John told me I would soon be as tall as he was. He added that if I continued eating mung beans like no other kid in the neighborhood; I would not need a chair to look out the window. Of course, my brother was trying to make me feel nice —the bounder. He wondered aloud what it would take to stop calling me an idiot.

I was speechless, waiting for John to elaborate.

"Show us how brave you are."

"How?"

"Imagine you are in the Olympics. First, jump off the chair."

I heaved off the chair to a standing ovation, and Ma joined in the applause as she came from the kitchen and stood at the partition.

After ensuring we were playing, she returned to Mr. Primus, our primus stove.

As Elisabeth snickered, John rattled off a list of furniture to jump from - the bed, the dining table, the teapoy, and his study table. I did these easily as my confidence rose with my newfound acceptance. Then, there was the challenging jump: a flying leap off the living-room cupboard, which was much taller than I was. I did it once while Ma and Narayan (our live-in helper) were in the kitchen.

I was impressed with Mr. Gabardine's concern as he removed the rolled-up mattresses our guests slept on atop the cupboard so I could stand flat. Like a langur, I clambered up the back of the armchair, deftly lifted myself onto the top, and stood up to my full height, touching the ceiling with my fingertips. Like a house lizard ready to snap its prey, I stood motionless, entirely focused. Ignoring the egging on from my siblings, I timed my jump like any Olympian worth his weight in precious metal; I leaped and landed unscathed. It was a breeze the second time. No more an idiot, I said to myself.

Not quite finished, John placed a rolled-up mattress on the cupboard and told me to have a go. He hoped I would quit, and I hurried up again and stood with my head inches from the ceiling. My wobbly feet dithered uncomfortably on the uneven mattress. My mind raced to the recent Marathi Hindu celebration of Janmashtami (Lord Krishna's birthday). A troupe enacted the story from Hindu mythology on the street below. They approached a large clay pot, strung over two stories high, singing 'Govinda Ala Ré Ala,' a lively Marathi song cautioning householders that Lord Krishna (aka Govinda) was on the prowl with his *Gopalas* (cowherds) to steal their buttermilk. A garland of paper money and flowers hung around the large clay pot, full of coins immersed in buttermilk, at the center of the rope strung thirty feet above the street, requiring five or six tiers of people to reach it. They smashed the pot to get at the coins using the shucked coconut, which served as the lid.

The bravest of them all, the bare-footed leader, ran up the human pyramid as if it were nothing. He looked like the conquering hero with his bright orange shirt and white headband. Only his shaky legs betrayed his trepidation as he stood on the shoulders of the two people below him. He tried several times to grab the garland of money, and finally, getting hold of it, he pulled the bunch free and pocketed it. He was now ready to smash the pot. As the crowd cheered him on, he swung the coconut. To the crowd's collective relief on the street and people like me watching the fun from the surrounding buildings, he hit the pot and broke it on his third attempt. The contents rained down the pyramid, and all the coins scattered everywhere as the crowd scampered to pocket them. The hero's clothes were no longer orange. Everyone forgot our dear leader as the pyramid collapsed in the ensuing melee. He went into free fall and broke his descent by sheer luck, grasping onto anything as he tested one of Newton's laws. Once he reached Earth, he seemed dazed by the experience of being on terra firma. The audience and his troupe were still fumbling around, preoccupied with the loose change. After regaining his wits, our leader took off with the money. Once his party realized he was gone, they took off after him.

I stood on the mattress, unsteady like a toddler, with the beat of Krishna's song rumbling in my head. I was about to make the leap of my life to please my oppressors. Besides sheer luck, I realized I needed the bravery shown by the leader of Lord Krishna's pyramid scheme. I took a deep breath, regretting not having practiced this variation of the cupboard jump. My audience seemed edgy and impatient, with John not pretending to hide the smirk on his face, and Elisabeth with an 'I-dare-you-look.' I took another deep breath, closed my eyes, and jumped at the count of three.

I crash-landed and doubled over in pain. My dominant left foot landed flat, but my right foot went askew. My luck had run out, and I knew my bravery was foolish. I sucked up my tears, caught my breath, and realized through the agony that I had at least tried the dare, unlike the two smug cowards, who I am sure would have never attempted my daring feat when they were my age.

"Hurry up, nurse, we have a problem," whispered John, impersonating a doctor, "The potten has done it again. Get the Iodex. Stat. Do not tell Ma."

"Yes, sir. Anything for the idiot," she replied.

John gently explored my foot and finally found the exact spot of my pain, and without missing a beat, the 'nurse' applied a generous amount of ointment. My brother rubbed it in, and I fainted, which alarmed them. As I drifted off, I realized they had used the potten and idiot monikers and reneged on our agreement. As I dragged myself gingerly for the next several days, I realized they never intended to keep their promise. Whenever Ma asked why I was shuffling, I quickly explained I had not had an egg in a long time. I did not feel like snitching on my siblings, and besides, it would be a treat if I could get a fried egg, a luxury in our home, out of the whole ordeal.

Besides teasing and belittling me at every turn, my siblings ordered me around to do their bidding: fetching stuff, polishing their footwear, and ironing their clothes. Dad wore trousers and coats with dog-eared cuffs, shirts with frayed collars, and unseasonal rubber rain shoes in the summer heat so my siblings could wear gabardine and silky skirts. Ma made do with threadbare saris and blouses with holes in the seams, and I with flapping soles.

One afternoon, as Elisabeth and I headed to Sunday school, my floppy sole caught the metal guard at the head of the concrete stairs. I tumbled headfirst down to the second floor, hitting the dozen or more stairs I do not recall the many times my head and back bounced off the stairs, when I reached the bottom, covered in bruises. I still remember with eidetic precision the undulating pulse of my sister's mocking laughter that followed me as I fell. I refused to cry and ran home to Ma, ashamed of myself. Elisabeth nonchalantly went to Sunday school. When Ma asked why she didn't help me home, her quick retort was that she didn't make me fall, and she felt she didn't have to bring me home because I had already run home. Aghast, Ma dressed her down and told her she had had enough of her backchat. My sister gave me a disgusted look as if I were to blame. Soon, I lost interest in Sunday school and all those tall stories. Dad taught me that addressing rude behavior was essential and that one should deal with it promptly because it only worsens over time. I do not think he ever heeded his advice, but unlike him, I kept an eye out for friendly combat.

My siblings and I did not regularly attend church because the services were in Malayalam. The liturgy was in a mixture of Malayalam and Syriac, and we had to remain standing during most of the two-hour service. Dad and Ma regularly attended when he held office. He had many detractors, mostly church members. The thorns in his side were a triumvirate of troublemakers. Fat Cherian was in cahoots with two other like-minded soulmates—KK and cock-eyed Varghese. KK, the stooping one, was ramrod tall, mustachioed with a military demeanor, and listened or pretended to with a tiresomely habitual stoop. Dad knew their tricks, and they knew Dad was the mastermind in thwarting them.

My parents were exceedingly tolerant. One look from Dad was enough to quell me. The disciplinarian was Ma, calm and cool, who always used a rolled-up newspaper instead of the first handy item. Even as mistrust of my siblings took root, I became a loner at home and school. I confided in my parents and discussed all matters with them, and they treated me as their best friend and confidant. Later, it helped when they turned to me for help, especially after my father's devastating accident, and my siblings were in medical college located out of state.

CHAPTER 1 PICTURES:

1. The small church in Kerala where my parents' marriage occurred in the 1930s (2023 photo).
2. John and Elisabeth at 7–9 months
3. I am at 12–15 months.

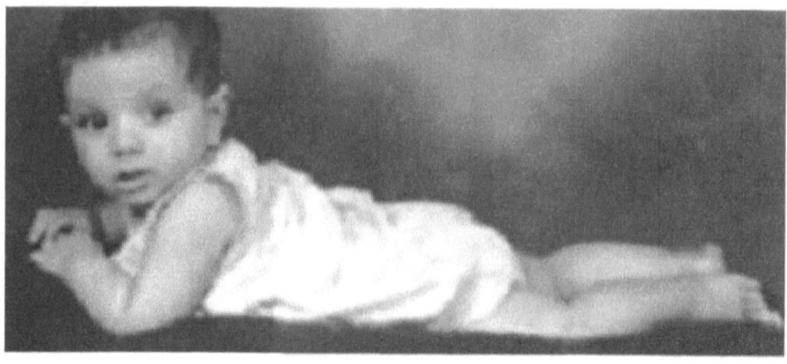

Chapter 2: Tenement Life

Sabita Building, a five-story tenement where we lived, was one of the tallest in our Dadar neighborhood. The 32 tenements (eight on each floor) with as many families (more than one hundred and fifty people) who lived in the building came from all over India and spoke different languages. The Daniel family and our guests, eight or nine of us in total, lived on the third floor in a one-room corner tenement.

Sabita and other such concrete structures were fortresses compared to the surrounding creaky, ready-to-crumble, multi-storied, gravity-defying wooden constructions that housed one of Bombay's economic engines—the cotton mill workers and their large families.

Buildings such as Sabita housed the Raj's clerks and professionals. Our neighbors were primarily Hindu families of various castes or *varnas*, speaking different languages. Many of them were the so-called highest-caste Brahmins. A Muslim family lived on our floor and spoke Urdu. We were one of three or four Christian families: Malayalam-speaking South Indian Orthodox Christians from Kerala, who, according to tradition, are among the oldest Christian communities in the world. Although the Hindus far outnumbered us, we lived amicably. I grew up amidst the cacophony of languages and religions and was the better for it. We celebrated each other's religious events, such as Diwali (a Hindu festival of lights), the Muslim celebrations of Ramadan and Eid al-Fitr, and Christmas. Our families exchanged sweets and other delicacies during these festivals.

Gray and drab, our building cried out for a fresh lick of paint, although it never got a paint job all the years I lived there. The west-facing windows of the tenement overlooked Main Road, the millworkers' dwellings, and the railway lines beyond. The tenement's north-facing windows faced the junction of Main Road and Naigaum Road. Kamath's restaurant, located across from us, had its radio set at high volume all day. During festivities, the mill workers celebrated by blasting the neighborhood with the latest songs through loudspeakers, the same few without reprieve. I had no way of avoiding Hindi movie songs, even if I wanted to, except when John shut all the windows, which made the noise unbearable while he studied. Although we did not have a radio like our neighbors, we had a gramophone with a few prized records.

Besides shops facing the Main Road like the other buildings, Sabita had two physicians with their dispensaries - one run by a young Parsee woman and another by an older Gujarati man. However, its most famous occupant was Sawant sahib, the notorious gang leader with two tenements above us who lived there with his two wives and many children. One of his tenements was directly above ours. He may also have had a third tenement below for his henchmen.

Sawant had the terrace under his lock and key for himself, his family, and his minions. Although his kids flew kites and played there at will, others like me were not so lucky. He once held an event with snacks and games for the rest of us. It was a place of intrigue for me—cloak and dagger stuff. As I entered the terrace, I was dazzled by the multi-colored inlaid-tile mosaic floor, and then my nostrils somersaulted at the all-pervading scent. Beyond the tiled floor in the cemented area stood the large water tanks with orange paint peeling from their sides, and further away were mounds covered with gunnysacks. His minions kept a wary eye on us while Sawant held court; one of them withered me with a glare and dispelled thoughts of any exploration. I am sure I had almost uncovered part of his *bewda* (moonshine) operation.

The street below provided much entertainment and some poignancy, which aroused my curiosity and concern. After waving Dad off most mornings, I watched the activities unfold below. The cobbled footpaths along the street were too narrow to contain all pedestrians. Unafraid of losing life or limb, they spilled onto the road, disregarding vehicular traffic. They comprised the tenement dwellers about their daily business, the street sweepers, and the merchants shouting out their wares and services: cobblers, newspaper recyclers, grinding-stone dressers, and the like.

Automobiles, including yellow-topped taxicabs and a fancy foreign car or two making their way to and from Ranjit Film Studio, lorries, bullock carts, hand-drawn carts, and Victorias (four-wheeled horse-drawn broughams), vastly outnumbered by pedestrians, trod carefully. Vendors with their four-wheeled carts occupied any remaining spaces with their wares—fruits, vegetables, and freshly roasted snacks like corn, peanuts, peas, and even kebabs. What was a curious boy to do from his third-floor vantage, sometimes well into the night, as he waited for his Dad?

Sabita stood east on Main Road, which ran north-south, North towards Matunga, and South towards Parel. It went north past the footbridge over the local and interstate railway lines connecting East and West Dadar, the railway station, Hindu Colony, King George High School, Ruia Arts and Science College, Podar Commerce College, and Matunga. South Main Road joined Vincent Road at the fork near Hindmata Cinema. Vincent Road went south past Parel to Victoria Terminus (Bombay's Fort district) and north to King's Circle with tramlines on its median. Chitra Cinema, located on Vincent Road, stood north of Hindmata. Tucked behind the cinema was a local Marathi Church that we Marthomites rented for Sunday school and services. The Jacobite Orthodox Church stood east of Vincent Road at the Naigaum crossroad. In 1889, the Malankara Syrian Church split into the Jacobite and Mar Thoma churches after a lawsuit awarded the Jacobites, the non-reformist tradition-bound group, most of the assets, and the reformist Marthomites ended up with a few churches in Travancore and precious little. However, these two groups, along with various denominations such as the Brethren and Pentecostals, take pride in their ancient roots. They are a garrulous, no-nonsense bunch, suspicious of others, not of their ilk, literalists to varying degrees, and secure in their piety.

Vincent Circle, now Khodadad Circle, was the place to be in Dadar with its bustling stores. We regularly frequented a few of them, often the Asiatic Agency, selling stationery, soaps, toothpaste, and assorted knick-knacks. Mr. Rao, who had a speech affliction, owned it. His voice rumbled out from the depths of his bowels in slow, strained monotones, which only Dad could understand. He was always there with his assistant, a young, bespectacled, newly arrived, Keralite. He took a liking to Elisabeth and sometimes asked me about her. Next-door was the Bata Shoe store, whose manager was a Malayali Jacobite whom Dad knew well. At the circle, Kurshed and Valia clothing stores, along with others, closed by nine, while the confectionery stores and restaurants bustled past 11 pm.

Each floor in Sabita had eight tiny quartz-floored tenements and a front veranda facing the street. The back verandas, with a staircase leading to the terrace, had two *moris* (washrooms), four *sandases* (toilets), a backdrop with a tall jambool tree, and miles away, Antop Hill in Wadala. My family, Narayan, and the two or three constant guests' living space on our lot consisted of a kitchen and a room partitioned into a living area and a bedroom, separated by thin plywood. A single, a double steel bed, and our versatile cracked marble-topped table, with two wooden folding chairs, stood in a U pattern. The narrow walkway connected it to the kitchen. Feng Shui could not have harmonized any better.

The living room, with its front veranda door, featured a couple of armchairs with wicker backs and seats, a teapoy, a cupboard, and John's study desk. Over his desk hung a framed magazine picture of Napoleon Bonaparte riding his men into battle against a leaden sky. The painting by Ernest Meissonier depicted Napoleon's 1814 Campagne de France. I remember Napoleon's beautiful white stallion and army on horseback, moving like a menacing juggernaut. I was appalled years later, thinking about my brother's hero-worship of Napoleon, of having Francisco de Goya's Tyrant of Europe enshrined. I would say this was a classic case of repressed megalomania. Then I am no Nietzsche.

Atop the three-shelved cupboard were mattresses for our guests. The top shelf held the HMV gramophone and John's collection of 78s. An unmatriculated cousin left it behind when Dad found him a job in Bahrain. Along with the timepiece, it was the object of my insatiable tinkering and curiosity about everything mechanical. This cousin loved his gramophone dearly, and years later, he took it back to Kerala, where it died when they ran out of needles. Our record collection languished for years after it lost its soulmate. Hefty hardbound accounting tomes that Dad used for his chit-fund business occupied the bottom shelf. When cricket became my passion years later, I used them for my picture collection of famous cricketers. The middle shelf contained knick-knacks, including a new addition— our first nail cutter, which became my set-me-free event. I could now do my own nails. There was no need to watch Ma pare my nails with the surgical scissors that were off-limits to me. I even made a tiny peephole in the plywood partition with its pointy file end and spied on the intruders who invaded our living room, visiting Dad with their endless problems as they whittled away my weekend with Dad.

Kids from my parents' families and their friends back home were matriculating at a fast clip. Initially in Madras and later in Bombay, Dad felt it was his duty to help their children after they passed high school. He was walking the talk from the Good Book. With his practice of helping beyond the self, Dad exhausted everyone around him, including Ma, although she was his willing accomplice. His salary was gone by the 15th of each month, and soon after, the borrowing began—to keep our temperamental Primus stove and the food chain going. He drained the joy out of John and Elisabeth as they came of age. The families from Kerala sought us out without fail, even those who had closer relatives than we, living in Bombay. Most of them showed up with nothing but the clothes on their backs. My parents considered it lucky to receive a postcard before their arrival, and these postcards often showed up days after they did.

———⊙———

WITH ITS TINY WASHROOM, the kitchen had a tap, more ornamental than functional. In all my years there, water hardly ever came through it. If it did, we looked at it with suspicion. The discolored water coughed and gurgled in spurts, and Ma quickly ended its misery by screwing it shut and wrenching the handle a second time. A large steel drum used to store water, a bit taller than me, stood next to our washroom. The drum was a bit of a luxury since not many in Sabita had one. I liked to stand on the washroom's parapet to look over the steel drum's rim and admire my reflection in the water. I shouted into its mouth to hear my voice reverberate.

My imagination ran wild with the different sounds I could make as the water level receded during the day. I often sang into the drum, hitting the sides for a beat. Like Dev Anand, I was the Taxi Driver and the retarded in *Funtoosh*. Like Raj Kapoor, I was the tramp in *Awara* (tramp) and the fraudster in Shree 420. The movie title referred to Section 420 of the Indian Penal Code. I bellowed like

Tarzan for Jane at the top of my lungs. My siblings, livid, with the kitchen booming with these sounds, screamed back that they could not focus.

"I'll fail SSC because of the idiot," my brother warned.

Elisabeth asked Ma whether they accepted idiots in the Thana asylum. Ma reasoned with me, explaining how important it was for John to pass the Secondary School Certificate Examination (SSCE) with a first class and get into Wilson College so Elisabeth could follow him. Right about then, John said Wilson was not in his plan; it was St. Xavier's College or nothing. Xavier's was one of the top colleges in the city. Elisabeth protested loudly; there was no way she would follow John. Sophia College for Women was her destination, which would be Sophia's or nothing. It was the top women's college in Bombay, and like Xavier's, it catered to the surrounding English-medium schools.

Moreover, John did not want to go to Wilson's because he did not want anything to do with our blowhard cousin, who had finished high school in Kerala with distinction a few years before John and had shown up at our place. Dad was so impressed with the cousin's grades that he eagerly borrowed and paid for the showoff's years at Wilson College.

After several minutes of this mayhem, my mother, wrestling with her Primus stove, got up. She pried my fingers one by one from the rim of the drum, shushed me, and offered me a book to read. I lay dejected after turning its pages. Hunger filled my stomach. When I could no longer stand it, I cried out to my lovely mother for help.

"I'm *brezek* Ma." Brezek was John's made-up word for hungry, which had become part of the Daniel family lexicon.

"My *ponnu moné* [precious son]," Ma said, "There's no kerosene for the primus stove. Let me get you cold water from the *matka* [earthen pot]." Water proved an indispensable backup in times like these.

It was past the middle of the month, and Dad was running later than usual.

"Ma, when will Dad be home?" I asked hopefully.

"Your father... he'll be here any minute. After that, we will get some kerosene from the *baniya* (grocer) so I can cook something nice for everyone. For once, we can eat together with Dad."

Most groceries belonged to baniyas from the Gujarati Marwari community, who monopolized the business. I wondered if the grocery store would be open when Dad came home. I could detect a strain in her voice and hoped she would not burst into tears as she often did when watching her hungry brood.

"I see a leg I can eat," said John playfully, eyeing me in mock seriousness. I was lying in the steel bed with my left leg dangling. Ma assured me he was only teasing and told him to quit.

The school had given me a glass of milk in the afternoon. Later at home, I retrieved the skin of the banana I had eaten, scraped the insides with a spoon, and shared some with Elisabeth. After that, Elisabeth chopped an onion and seasoned it with salt, and the two of us devoured it, pretending it was *Bhel-Puri*, a Bombay street food. Besides the onion and salt, everything else was missing in Elisabeth's rendition: the puffed rice, *sev* or lentil-based crunchy noodles, crushed purees, chutney, tamarind water, diced mango, boiled potato, tomato, chilies, cilantro, and some intangibles like the dust and grime of Bombay. The onion would have tasted better with lemon juice. However, we had not seen the backside of one in a while.

Ma's sad eyes told the story as she looked up and turned away to hide the tears, muttering, "Lord, why is he so late? Could he not find someone to borrow from? Did You send him off on another mission? When does he think of these hungry souls? When Jesus? Does he not know that our starving children are waiting? Did You have to teach Your lessons so well that he forgets his own and runs around helping others every night? Lord, how can I watch them munching rock salt and onions, tell me?" Her clenched, helpless fists relaxed as she turned toward me.

"Son, go read so you'll stand first again. He'll be here any minute."

"You promise?"

"Yes, I promise. I'll send Narayan for kerosene."

Narayan helped Ma with some of her chores. He took me to school, brought me home, took the tiffin lunches for John and Elisabeth at their schools, and ran other errands. Narayan lived with us. My parents also gave him a monthly salary, which he dutifully sent to his family back home. He was much older than me, although I had to teach him the ropes of living in our big city.

"Ma, can you buy just one egg and fry it, too? I forget what an egg tastes like. Promise to share it." The Muslim egg merchant also sold single eggs.

"We'll see when Dad's home."

She did not sound reassuring.

Wall geckos skittered and stopped looking for flies since the dispirited flies had tucked themselves in for a hungry night ahead on the three grimy wires that ran to the bare bulbs in our tenement. Hunger battered my belly in waves. Finally, there was relief as I drifted into my own cocoon. It was dark when I woke up to my parents talking while Narayan was out to get kerosene and an egg. Things were even worse for these so-called low-caste Hindus in Kerala, like Narayan. After dropping out after a year or two of school, they had no livelihood, no future. My parents had taken him in, another mouth to feed. I think of it now as collective misery for all of us at 24, Sabita.

Soon, the distinctive smell of South Indian asafetida-based lentil-vegetable stew called *Sambhar* permeated the tenement, and the chili powder from the frying potato chips tickled my nostrils.

Some green mango pickle and *Samandhi podi* (chutney powder) would also be available. Ma had kept her promise of something nice to go with the rice. I was happy, although there was no egg smell.

Suddenly, we heard children and women screaming. The water in the two taps in the main washroom had started, and it was time to fill our water drum. They turned on the water from the tanks on our building's terrace late in the evenings, though not at a set time. Today, it happened before our delayed meal. Ma dropped everything when the water games started. All eight families had to collect water since it lasted only a few minutes. I nearly passed out again, waiting to eat.

Like clockwork, an invisible hand turned on the water. Screaming and clapping with relief, the exuberant women and older children scrambled to get to the taps. Some brought water hoses to connect the faucets and placed unimaginable containers to catch the leaks. They saved every drop they could, although there was no getting around a leaky process. The floor, wet from all the leaks, was slippery, and everyone had to be careful in the dimly lit area. Not everyone had water hoses; those who did freely shared them. It was at least a two-person job. While one stood guard at the tap, the other rolled out the hose to their tenement to collect the water in steel drums, buckets, or other containers. Ma, at first, fell to her knees. She thanked *Yeshu Christu* for turning on the water and took her time. My brother would usually pipe in here, telling her to cut out 'Yeshu' and thank Sawant sahib instead.

Besides all the criminal activities he was involved in, he controlled the water supply in the building. He had all the families in Sabita Building in his pocket. He ensured that every floor received its daily water supply for approximately 30 minutes. Sometimes, that invisible hand strayed and shut off the water before the time was up, to noisy protests from everyone. At other times, the same hand allowed the water supply to continue. Rumors were floating that

Sawant sahib even had running water in one of his tenements by some quirk of fate. Ma remained convinced Jesus loved everyone, including Hindu gangsters.

Sawant sahib's various children included Kamala, a few months older than me, who sometimes played with us. His oldest son, Ravi, who was as old as my brother, nodded when we passed.

Although a seemingly devout Maratha Hindu, Sawant sahib had no use for monogamy and cast aside these inconveniences. Sawant's activities included moonshine, *Matka* (numbers betting), and *charas* (drugs). The police and politicians were also in his pocket. Since his minions worked after dusk, they hung around Sabita all day and inadvertently protected us.

Ma had them all in mind when she talked to Him. Sometimes, I wondered about Ma. How could she be so clever and yet so crazy pious? I know this: she was as genuine as the mole at the center of my neck. She had much too much on her mind. The worst of it was trying to keep our bodies and souls together. She did all the thankless tasks in our household. She cared for Narayan, the relatives who constantly cycled through our home throughout my childhood, and us. While the job seekers were in her charge, she ensured they followed some rules, such as Dad's instructions. We were among the few families at Sabita who subscribed to the Times of India. He required them to read the front page of the newspaper aloud. Ma corrected their stammering English and asked them to paraphrase what they'd read to her in Malayalam and English. It helped in their forthcoming interviews. Ma did not allow Narayan to sit idly by and laugh at this often funny but torturous process. Ma taught him to read and write Malayalam. I, too, got interested in the newspaper, first the Sunday comics and later R. K. Laxman's daily cartoons.

The newcomers sometimes stayed for weeks, and many stayed for months and months. My siblings thought of them as parasites, and in retrospect, I don't blame them. To me, they were always playmates.

Many left Ma in tears, angry that they had to vacate shortly after finding a job. They got in a lick or two before they slammed the door on her. Others showed up after church on Sundays. The nurses breezed in with a whiff of talcum powder and perfume, little maps of sweat in the armpits of their tight new blouses, and a newly acquired spring in their steps, looking like they had received a well-deserved dose of self-confidence. Some of the boys came with the smell of cigarettes on their breath. They no longer looked like the wastrels who showed up at our door a few months earlier. John and Elisabeth ignored them while I jostled with them. To be truthful, I enjoyed their visits and looked forward to their coming. My parents welcomed them all. They came empty-handed with a big appetite for Ma's mouth-watering meals. Ma made sure they would come back again.

⎯⎯⎯◉⎯⎯⎯

IN COMPARING KERALA with other Indian states, the environmentalist Bill McKibben described Kerala as a bizarre anomaly. It was anything but that. Let me say this about 'God's Own Country'—her ascendancy was no fluke. Decades before India's independence in 1947, free primary and high school education, along with improved access to basic healthcare, were cornerstones in Travancore as it advanced and left the rest of India behind. The British needed many matriculates to run their vast machinery. Travancore was at the forefront of this effort. After they left in 1947, Travancore's ascendancy continued. Colleges sprouted everywhere, charging only nominal fees. Travancore marched on towards 100% literacy. By 1991, the literacy rate in Kerala was over 90 percent. Even though Travancore was rapidly industrializing during its last ruler's reign from 1931 to 1949, jobs could not keep pace with the exploding number of matriculated youngsters. They left Travancore in droves rather than hang around wading through rice fields, tapping rubber, or climbing coconut trees. Jobs awaited them in India's principal port cities: Madras, Bombay, and Calcutta. The state is now about 55 percent Hindu, 20 percent Christian, and 20 percent Muslim. In Travancore, the groups mostly tolerated each other, unlike elsewhere in India. Self-serving politicians in other states sometimes stoked communal trouble, resulting in deadly riots between Hindus and minorities. One cannot say that Travancore was a kind of utopia where religions and customs mingled seamlessly. Despite its checkered history concerning the oppressed, many of her visionary rulers and leaders saw pervasive poverty as the common enemy rather than ethnic and religious differences. Education was the key to fighting it, and diversity was helping rather than hindering progress.

———◉———

DAD WAS AMONG THE FIRST from Travancore to move to Bombay in the 1930s. He was an avid reader. His helpful ways and copious knowledge earned him well-deserved recognition and admiration from many. After airing their seemingly insoluble problems, Dad's visitors listened and heeded his advice and counsel. They often stayed for tea and loud political debates, eroding Ma's welcome and my patience.

According to my brother, Dad's friends who visited us before my time were M. Padmanabhan, an Independence activist and Social reformer; V. K. Krishna Menon, first Defense Minister of India; and E. M. S. Namboodripad, Kerala's first Chief Minister. Padmanabhan, the senior-most, was the revered one. Dad knew them before they became politicians and officeholders. If I were to guess, they became friends when their paths crossed as members of the Indian Congress Party. All four, including Dad, the youngest and probably the most well read, were quite active and spoke at public rallies during the heady days of our freedom struggle. After Gandhi returned to

Bombay from South Africa, the city became a hub of political discourse, and many leaders visited him. When his movement went national and touched villages across India's vastness, he sometimes visited Bombay. I was not around or too young to know many of Dad's friends.

Well-known people and others who were less well-known frequently visited our tenement while I was growing up. Dad's best friend, Mr. Joseph John, a fellow Marthomite, had a BA in English and started as a stenotypist for K. M. Munshi, a political activist, educator, and environmentalist. Like Dad, Joseph was well read. He took his passion for photography to another level. Like Dad, Joseph also wrote books. Joseph later worked as a journalist and was the principal of Bhavan's College of Mass Communications. He sometimes came to our home, but usually met Dad at church, the library, and Congress Party events. Joseph arrived in Bombay around the same time as Dad. I remember him showing up early one morning at our tenement with a cube-shaped camera. One of the photographs I still have is of my brother, standing blissfully half-asleep with his long, skinny fingers wrapped around my parents' shoulders. Joseph's son sent me a photo recently, one I had never seen before of my sassy sister and me. In the early sixties, Dad and Joseph were also members of the forward-looking Friends of the Trees (FOT) organization. Joseph was one of its founding members and recruited Dad. We thoroughly enjoyed all their annual tree-huggers exhibitions (featuring orchids, trees, flowers, and vegetables) held at Raj Bhavan in Bombay, the official residence of the Governor of Bombay. FOT participated in many activities, including planting saplings in and around Bombay.

━━━━●━━━━

AFTER INDEPENDENCE in 1947, Travancore was under central government rule until 1957. Almost nine years later, in 1956, the

Malayalam-speaking areas of Travancore and its surrounding regions merged to form the state of Kerala. Famously known as 'God's Own Country,' Kerala is scenic in its natural state with its endless sea-leaning coconut trees on its emerald coastline, white sand beaches, lagoons, backwaters, and breathtaking flora and fauna.

E. M. S. Namboodripad (EMS for short) had changed political parties by then. At the forefront of land reform changes in Kerala, EMS's party won the most votes in Kerala's first-ever elections. He became Kerala's first chief minister-elect with a coalition of five independent parties. EMS offered Dad a position in his council of ministers, and Dad politely declined. Dad would have had to return to Kerala if he had accepted the job. As it turned out, it would have been quite an upheaval for nothing. EMS's government lasted two years, after which the center took over the state's administration following mass protests that forced EMS's resignation. He spent 12 years in the political wilderness before returning as Chief Minister.

Based on his outstanding civic work, Dad was one of thirteen volunteer members selected to serve on the Consumers' Advisory Committee of the Government of Bombay during the state's rationing years, from the early 1940s to the mid-1950s. They advised the government about the fair distribution of staple food items in short supply. As a result, Dad met people in high positions at various government entities, hospitals, and companies. He sought them out relentlessly, canvassing shamelessly for openings for the youngsters from Travancore. He found nurse-training jobs for women and clerical or factory jobs for matriculated and un-matriculated boys. Some were not even our relatives. My parents helped Mary, who was unrelated to us and always super friendly. She stayed with us when she first came to Bombay before I was born. Matron Mary, my godmother, was also one of Ma's best friends. She visited us often and would always bring her godson something. More than anything else, her smile and all the positive energy, she brought with her lit me up. Uncle George worked for the Times of India as a supply clerk. He lived in Bandra, a district predominantly populated by Goan Catholics, renowned for their pork dishes. His Goan Catholic landlady taught him to make mouth-watering Pork Vindaloo, and he regularly brought us some. Kerala Christians did not generally eat pork; however, Uncle George's pork dishes were tasty and a welcome change to our meat-deprived diet.

Dad and Ma talked about the exceptions, such as Uncle George, Aunt Sara, and Matron Mary, who stood by us through the thick and most of the thin. Although they were not blood relatives, we shared a mutuality that bound us. When I went to Kerala as a child, I remember a long bus ride from Ma's home to meet Uncle George's and Aunt Sara's widowed mother, who surprised us with a grand feast.

Often, on a Thursday afternoon, when I had a half-day off from school, we would visit Mary, our relatives, and other good friends around Bombay. Of course, most of these were unannounced visits since no one we knew had a phone. Ma hemmed and hawed over me for these month-end visits, making me look my best in the one pair of outside clothes I had, a cream-colored shirt with an eye-pleasing contrasting pair of dark brown shorts. In hindsight, I can only guess why we made these regular visits. I looked forward to these trips to see my mother's friends and relatives, have their snacks and tea, and ride the train or the red-and-white colored double-decker buses operated by the Bombay Electric Supply & Tramways Company (BEST Co.). It meant standing on a twinkling machine with a flashing red light while waiting at the platform for the train to Bandra. After putting a coin in it, the little zebra-painted disk went round and round, and the machine whirred into action, magically punching out a little cardboard piece that told me my weight and future. I marveled at that machine and wondered how it worked, although I was stuck at forty pounds forever.

In addition to these visits, Ma steeped us in Kerala culture and Hindu mythology, ensuring we absorbed it in abundance. Elisabeth and I accompanied Ma to Malayalam plays and poetry recitals by *maha kavis* (great poets). She often took us to see Bharatanatyam and Kathakali, two famous Indian classical dances performed by renowned South Indian artists. More often than not, we gatecrashed and sat in the front row; I watched the artists light the two oil-dipped wicks of the tall floor lamp at the front of the stage. I fell in love with the Travancore Sisters and the Kerala Sisters. I was in awe of their beauty, dainty, doll-like body movements, and sheer energy. Their expressive, sparkling, almond-shaped, kohl-lined eyes, in complete sync with the music and vocals in the background, held me totally in their spell as they danced out stories from Hindu mythology to the accompaniment of Carnatic music and live singing. Due to my limited Malayalam vocabulary, I did not understand the stories sung. Above the din, Ma explained the mythology to me as best as possible, earning her some Kathakali-type glares from grown-ups sitting near us. As the music and the vocals died down, the dancers made the Anjali Mudra or namaskar gesture and gently snuffed out the lamp. It was a fitting climax to the stories as they stepped back, palms held together in a farewell *namasté*, one dainty step back at a time, in keeping with the fading tinkle of the time-keeping *gungaroos* (anklet bells) used in Indian classical dancing.

During Passion Week, she would often take us to the church grounds every evening for prayers and testimonies from the congregants. Then came the evening's highlight—a revival sermon by the *ubadeshi* (lay preacher), who never failed to bore us to tears and scare us to death about what awaited us if we chose not to save ourselves in time. Sitting beside me with a sad face, Ma got up, tears streaming down her cheeks, chanting 'amen, amen' and blabbering with the rest of the crowd every time the lay preacher paused for effect. To our amazement, one preacher even pointed out the exact location of heaven in the starlit sky. On the makeshift stage, the light from the bright bald bulb suffused his talcum-plastered face when he tilted his head toward the sky. At that moment, he let the oceans of tears he had held back stream down his cheeks. The crowd buzzed; many, including me, turned around and looked at heaven's newly discovered home. It was quite a dramatic ending to the evening. I believed him until Dad rolled his head and twinkled his eyes like a Kathakali dancer in disbelief. On our way home, I imitated the preacher's actions and words, repeatedly jabbing the sky toward the latest sighting of heaven, until my family burst out laughing. Suddenly, Ma stopped laughing as she prayed, eyes pinched shut, facing heaven. She prayed fervently and loudly, imploring Him to forgive their sacrilege so they could avoid the dire consequences that awaited them.

⸻ ◉ ⸻

JOHN WAS AN EXCEPTIONAL kid. At eleven, he published a story in Shankar's Weekly, a children's magazine. Writing and publishing short stories throughout his school and college years, and beyond, became his passion. Attention! Flying Saucers over Gironde, a short story John wrote, set in France during a time when flying saucer sightings were all the talk, is one I recall. He came home with arms full of prize books during his school years. As I turned the pages in awe, I imagined the stories from the pictures, since I didn't have the knack for reading like my siblings. They howled like hyenas without correcting me as I stammered through my mispronunciations. I never understood why fairy tale books, especially the Granny Series, with pleasant enough stories, had big-nosed old women on the covers to scare people like me.

His high school final year examination, the SSCE, was in March; it was 'SSC' this and 'SSC' that, all year long. Students took tests in English, French, Algebra and Geometry, Physics and Chemistry, General Science, and Geography at a state-assigned school. Above 60 percent was first-class. Students who score below 33% in a subject have the option to retake the subject in October or retake the entire exam in March. Either way, you lost a year if going to college was the plan. St. Xavier's and Elphinstone were the top two colleges in Bombay, and Xavier's became his focus. He got a first-class with more than enough marks to get into Xavier's. To his chagrin, Dad enrolled him in Wilson College so John and his cousin could attend college together. I don't think John and Elisabeth liked him much because when the cousin first lived with us for months, he was a bloviating showoff and an even bigger tattler. At Wilson College, John disliked our cousin's paternal attitude towards him, hated the college, and frequently skipped classes. He barely made it through his first year but passed the university exams the following year with a third-class degree, which ruined his chances of getting into medical college that year. Even though John wanted to be a writer, Dad argued that he should become a professional and write on the side. All my brother had to do was look around the Sabita neighborhood to understand Dad. After the cousin left Wilson with a Chemistry degree, John coaxed Dad into moving him to St. Xavier's College for his Junior BSc year. He performed well that year and got into medicine without a hitch.

━━━━◉━━━━

DAD AND MA TOOK CENTER stage with their incredible love, trust, and respect for each other and others, doing great works of compassion for their relatives and friends without any expectations. Beyond the fact that we read a good deal and did well in school, activities that required any expense fell by the wayside. My siblings figured it out long before I did. I thought nothing about the 'hand-to-mouth' existence we led because I knew no better. It was like the imaginary Bhel-Puri my sister conjured up when we were hungry. I am sure we were practicing to be pretenders in an elaborate scene of Barmecide's feast, named after a prince in The Arabian Nights. If there was a God, he had to be like Barmecide, providing a hoax of a meal at first, and after our pretense of being sated, he laid out the grand banquet. We could always count on a bellyful of hope and a bit of dumb luck.

CHAPTER 2 PICTURES:

1. My parents and John.
2. Elisabeth and me
3. The tenement picture where I lived until I was nine, photographed in 2009. The print book's

back cover features a tenement as the background, along with my photo, bio, and testimonials.

Joseph John, one of Dad's best friends, photographed both pictures. He arrived at our tenement on a weekend (probably a year or two before Dad's accident, when he still had his left hand) when we were barely awake. You can see John was still a bit sleepy. Behind John is the infamous cupboard with the rolled-up mattresses from which I jumped a few years earlier.

Chapter 3: Schooled by the Streets

Notwithstanding the abundance of activity at home, they were no match for the activities outside, in Sabita, and on the street below. John once pointed out and named a schoolmate passing by our tenement. He hid behind me while I continued to call his friend. Finally, Rusi looked up and waved back. Rusi Surti, a southpaw whose career I followed for years, became one of India's finest cricketers.

The kitchen's double windows had one window bolted shut. It limited the number of hungry crows jostling for a better view of Ma's kitchen from the window ledge. These clever, beady-eyed Corvids hung around waiting to strike and cawed at Ma's every move. Ma once caught a crow 'red-handed' in the kitchen. We ate crow for lunch that day. It tasted bitter, possibly due to their scavenging ways; it was a welcome change since we had not eaten meat in a while. Ma cooked it well because none of us fell ill. Her nursing background was handy, even though we all lived in the same one-room tenement and did not get sick as often as our neighbors. When John came down with typhoid—a food and waterborne contagion—Ma and Dad knew we might all catch it. Ma diagnosed it correctly, tucked her sari's *pallu* (hanging end) into her midriff, and worked like Florence Nightingale. With John still sick and awaiting hospital admission, she took numerous precautions. She kept us away from him and boiled everything. I mean everything. She was determined to avoid another casualty, which she did. John finally went to the hospital for treatment. After his quick recovery, he returned home to a hero's welcome.

John referred to the toilet area as the bogs. With half-buckets of precious water, Ma made futile attempts to overcome the stench caused by some of our neighbors who uncaringly urinated in the bathroom beside the bogs. For this reason, we bathed in our kitchen washroom, and whenever we bathed, Ma and Narayan moved the kitchen work to the bedroom table.

Eight families shared the bogs with the four stalls' unsightly keyhole-shaped porcelain floor-level toilets. The keyhole side of the toilet connected to the discharge drainpipe, which contained the flotsam from the previous flush. I was deathly scared of them and imagined it was only a matter of time before the keyhole swallowed me whole. The flushes seldom worked, and I was sure my plight was a lifetime one. Hoping to get lucky, I gave the chain a mighty tug before running home to safety in the slippers my parents had insisted I wear outside the tenement.

While the other children's fathers were home by six, Dad never did. I often looked out the windows to see Dad make his grand appearance. Usually, he had a tome tucked under his arm, which meant that he visited the library in addition to visiting our former houseguests at their hospitals to ensure they were well. When I spotted Dad, I repeatedly shouted, '*Achachan veranu*' (Dad is coming), berserk with relief. I waved vigorously, hoping he would see me. When he saw me, I repeatedly screamed '*Achachan kandu*' (Dad has seen). Passersby on the street looked up and wondered at all the commotion; some even mistakenly waved back. Ma rushed from the kitchen and stood by, waving at them. Sometimes, everyone, including guests, joined us.

As soon as Dad saw us, he waved back with gusto, and he felt like a rock star, given the large crowd at the window. As Dad looked up and scanned the many faces, I was sure he was only looking for me. He made me feel special; we probably all felt the same way. He kissed

Elisabeth and me when he breezed in, smiling as Ma stood by, letting her resolve to scold him for his late arrival fade away.

"*Edi koché* [dear child], what is there to eat?" he invariably asked. "I am brezek." Ma blushed at such terms of endearment. He sometimes belted out words of a popular Malayalam movie song called *Vishap Inde Villi* (Cry of the Hungry). He often sang English and Malayalam hymns and made-up songs about Ma's sister-in-law and Cruella, mostly while bathing—boisterous and utterly tuneless. He also practiced speeches, often reciting the Gettysburg Address and Nehru's Independence Day speech. He knew only a few lines but continued impromptu. That was my Dad, the irrepressible singer and elocutionist.

Achachan, my mother would invariably say, 'if you were so hungry, why don't you show up at six like the other dads? Your son refuses to sleep until he sees you striding home. If *Otta Kaiyan* [the one-handed man] comes around, he shouts at the poor man. What good is it for Mathew to see them bullying the poor man?'

Otta Kaiyan was the village idiot, except that this was no village, and he was no idiot. Life was unfair to him. To me, there was a sad inevitability in his circumstance. I always felt sorry for him, although I could not do much because I was a seven-year-old with my own problems. I usually watched him from my perch at the window, though Ma and I encountered him on the street one fateful morning. I winced. He was severely handicapped, with a missing right arm and a face that had collapsed on one side. I shuddered at his disfigurement as Ma tugged at me. Years later, I remember what went through my mind when I stood transfixed. I was like Scout, the hero of To Kill a Mockingbird, who came face to face with scary Boo, the neighbor. Instead of turning away, I stood unflinching and took in the scene. His complexion was ruddy from spending so much time in the sun in front of restaurants and grocery stores, looking for something to eat. He had worn-out shoes with flapping soles. His ankles were grimy with dirt. He wore trousers at least a size too large and had rolled the legs up to his calves. He tucked his oversized shirt loosely into his pants, held together by a rope through the belt loops. The cutout sleeve of his shirt hung lifelessly where his arm should have been. He wore a straw hat pulled down tightly over his head. With his big, sad eyes, the left more prominent than the right, he saw me and smiled to reassure me he was harmless.

He addressed me in Hindi as a child and asked why I was staring at him. He told me not to be afraid, and he was just another being like me. Taking his hat off, he curtsied like Raj Kapoor in Awara. Raj Kapoor was a charismatic Hindi film actor known for his movie Awara (The Tramp), which featured him curtsying like Charlie Chaplin every chance he got.

"*Aré* [Hey] Otta Kaiyan, you are an awara like Raj Kapoor," I yelled, finding my voice in broken Hindi over the din of the street. I was sure Otta Kaiyan did not know the Malayalam words for 'one-handed man,' which was a mistake I relived years later. He agreed he was an awara and reminded me he was not a mere kid like me. He waved goodbye with a smile and wished Allah would go with us. He was probably a *Musulman* (Muslim) from North India. My parents had taught me by example that people were only people; it did not matter where one came from or who one was.

Whenever I spotted Otta Kaiyan on the street, I hoped he would vanish before Sawant sahib's minions picked on him. He had a knack for showing up at the wrong time. One of Sawant's scoundrels would approach him and say something insulting, and another would come from behind and pull his rope belt.

Otta Kaiyan shouted, "Hey, you son of a cobbler."

"You called me a cobbler's son?" a hoodlum would ask, trying to whack OK's hat off.

His only hand alternated between holding on to his hat and the rope belt.

"You, mothereffer, go pull off your sister's skirt, you bastards."

Passersby dared not admonish the harassers but gathered around him, their eyes wide with gleeful anticipation. Once, when a hoodlum pulled at his ragged clothing, OK shrieked and sank his teeth into the intruder.

"Are you a bloody dog?" yelled the minion. "You know how we treat dogs, don't you?"

We had plenty of dogs in our neighborhood, all of them stray and abused. A cohort then held Otta Kaiyan down while the aggrieved punched him several times, and he doubled over with each blow and fell on the ground, cursing. The onlookers guffawed shamelessly as the scene unfolded on the street below my window. Someone familiar bellowed from the fourth floor, a few feet above me. It was Sawant sahib himself.

"Hey, Chottu, that's enough. Stop teasing and get him some water, and if I catch you again, watch it," he thundered. He was angry when he told Chottu to cut it out; I recognized an underlying threat. They dispersed after Chottu shoved a glass of water from Kamath's restaurant into Otta Kaiyan's outstretched hand. Whenever Sawant sahib was around, he looked out for OK. He always stopped the foolery when it got out of hand.

Bemused at first, I watched with deepening concern. My stomach doubled with every blow as I watched helplessly, runnels of tears flowing freely. Ma rushed to help me from my chair, but I would not, not before I saw Otta Kaiyan throw the glass. It rang Chottu's bell, stunning him cold. Hurt and humiliated, Chottu dragged himself towards Sabita Building, rubbing his noggin, muttering.

Sawant sahib bellowed again, "Take that glass back to Kamath sahib. Say sorry for the commotion in front of his business." Chottu, mumbling under his breath, gathered the glass and shuffled to the restaurant. Meanwhile, Otta Kaiyan refused any help from the crowd, and he got up, brushed himself off, and left, cursing.

I sighed with relief, knowing that Otta Kaiyan was the bravest man in my world. To show this much courage and chutzpah against such odds impressed me. Even with Sawant hitting the brakes, it was a tragic sight. In my heart, I thanked him for his timely action.

I could not have guessed then that OK would inadvertently play a big part in my life.

When I went to school, I sometimes saw Sawant sahib on the street, heatedly gesticulating and bossing his simpering minions. Rumor had it that he had even knifed his enemies. Yet, the man and his gangsters operated openly. He was the only one in the building who owned a chauffeur-driven car. He was about my father's height, a heavy-set, muscle-bound dude who wore starched white pants and a full-sleeved shirt. He rolled his sleeves up to the middle of his sculpted forearms. He left a couple of the top buttons of his shirt undone, revealing a thick gold necklace and a fistful of curly black hair. He matched it all with stunning *Kolhapuris* (handcrafted, gold-braided, vegetable-tanned leather footwear made in Kolhapur). His eyes were often bloodshot, and his face and neck were tide-marked with talcum powder. He combed back his well-oiled, wavy black hair with no parting.

Otta Kaiyan, Sawant, his minions, and others helped me understand my world better. I could see that, despite the stark contrasts and stations in life, such as between Sawant and Otta Kaiyan, Sawant prevented a grave wrong from happening through his presence and sense of fairness, even though he was a ruthless gangster. Life had so many angles that so confounded me. I wish it were predictable—black and white, without any gray, easy to understand. I knew I would have to grow up fast.

Chapter 4: Daily Rush Hour

Unlike Tolstoy's unhappy families, ours was happy despite our circumstances. Amidst the quiet desperation ran a stream of optimism grounded in truth and confidence that Dad and Ma espoused. I watched family history making and learned how families stayed together and came apart. It was all about mutuality, and Ma was the clear-eyed captain at the prow. Weekdays, including Saturdays, were hectic, as busy as the Flora Fountain roundabout in downtown Bombay, except that all the congestion occurred in a space of less than 250 square feet.

Dad was a head clerk at BPT Railways. His office, located at Ballard Pier, close to downtown, opened at 10 a.m. To reach work involved a 20-minute local train ride to Victoria Terminus (VT) from Dadar and a ten-minute hike to the office. Ma's first big job was getting Dad off to work every morning. He started the day with a quick scan of the newspaper headlines, a dash to the toilet, and a bath in the kitchen washroom. Ma and Narayan, busy as woodpeckers, scurried back and forth from the kitchen to our dining table when we (except me) had a bath.

Dad's off-key songs and the urgency of the cawing crows would get Ma rattled enough to bang on the door when Dad took too long. Dad and the crazy crows continued merrily, ignoring her. Ma kept knocking until he responded.

"Dear child, what is it?" he would ask. She had no time to blush.

"Hurry up. My ears are exploding. Everyone is waiting, sir."

He emerged from the kitchen, muttering, wrapped in a towel because Ma called him out.

"I can't even bathe in peace," he complained, feigning annoyance. We all huddled in the bedroom, waiting, as Dad dressed in the front room where Ma had laid out his clothes.

"There would be Satyagraha if you had taken any longer," Ma would retort, invoking Gandhi's non-violent resistance movement to make the point. John, too, got in on the act. He announced in the manner of a politician, "There, ladies and gentlemen, Mrs. Daniel advocates Satyagraha. Pray, what does it all mean? At best, it is a malapropism. At worst, it is a call to sedition and open mutiny. Be careful, Ma; these walls have ears, especially our neighbor's long, pointed ones." He was referring to Mr. Deshmukh, our Brahmin neighbor.

After struggling with his clothes and shoes, Dad showed up from the living room without John's predicted results in his play-by-play commentary. After a quick breakfast and hurried kisses, Dad was out the door and on his way. I waved to him from the window as he strode off.

Ma had much more to do after sending off Dad. She and Narayan were back at our dining table cleaning the rice, cutting vegetables, and whatnot to get the next meal ready—our lunches—as John hummed his way through his bath.

Ma was banging on the kitchen door again.

"*Yohanan*, come out this minute."

When Ma called John by the Aramaic version of his name, as in the Malayalam bible, you knew she was upset.

"I just got in."

"No arguments. I am counting to 10."

He was out before 10.

"Come, Elisabeth, your turn. Here is your school uniform."

"Ma, I don't want to bathe today." She had a phobia of soap and water.

"Whether you want to or not is beside the point. You get in there and hurry up. No Daniel will step out of my house without a bath, and that's how it is."

Elisabeth called out when she finished; Ma rushed to inspect and help her with her clothes. My bath could wait until Ma finished with the *dabbawalla* (tiffin carrier), a matter more pressing than sending off my Dad and siblings on time. I called out to my siblings from my window as they went to school in formation, John leading Elisabeth. Sometimes, they rewarded me by waving back.

Next on Ma's list was the tiffin carrier, our humble, overworked Bombay icon. Our tiffin carriers were admired worldwide for their near-perfect execution of delivering thousands of lunches through rain or sun throughout the Bombay office area—clearly, Six Sigma at its finest, perhaps even before the term's invention. National Geographic Magazine memorialized them some years ago. Even Prince Charles came to see them in action. Uncharacteristically, though, the British did not take any credit for this one jewel in their crown. Ma had to prepare Dad's lunch and have it waiting outside the door, in the stacked round metal containers, every day on time. At the same time, she prepared lunches for John and Elisabeth, and Narayan delivered them to their schools after dropping me off at the Montessori.

Three events usually gummed up Ma's kitchen operations. Primarily, Ma ran out of money to feed Mr. Primus Stove's addiction to kerosene. Secondly, Mr. Primus's volatility added to Ma's woes. Finally, yet importantly, the grinding stone and its mate, the stone rolling pin, went on strike after they became too bald with wear.

Mr. Primus knew he was the only game at 24, Sabita, and acted out his whims on poor Ma and Narayan. The kerosene in Mr. Primus's belly came from a four-gallon container tucked under the spice table. I could tell the state of Ma's kitchen by how much kerosene remained. As the month wore on, so did the amount of kerosene. Two weeks into the month, I could usually lift the container myself. Everything halted by the 20th when the can was empty. Ma invoked the Almighty to spare us this one time so her hungry youngest one, me, could eat before he fell asleep. She often pleaded with Mr. Primus as he died with a big grunt while the rice was still half-cooked. He timed his death rattle perfectly and knew he was the source of all our succor and nourishment. He demanded respect from Ma and Narayan, as he occupied the center spot on Ma's kitchen floor, just like the Bharatanatyam floor lamp. My classical dance experiences were handy as I watched the well-synced pair in action.

One of them knelt down and first cleared Mr. Primus's nozzle with an instrument that had a unique pin at its tip. Then, they lovingly garlanded the nozzle with the crescent-shaped metal-wrapped cotton igniter dipped in denatured spirit. The spirit was contained in a dark, translucent bottle with a skull-and-crossbones emblem and 'POISON' across the scary picture. Still on their knees, while one of them stroked the pump and fed his belly with fresh air, the other finally opened the valve slightly and lit the garland. If the genuflections and the pleas to Mr. Primus's good nature were proper, with no missteps or groans, he coughed and sputtered to life as the atomized kerosene lit up. It was sheer relief that I saw writ on their glowing faces. When they helped each other in this manner, and Mr. Primus performed well, exhibiting a bluish flame, the pair stepped back like my Kerala Sisters. As I admired their well-timed moves, I swear I heard the jingle of the anklet bells and the rapidly fading music as they synced each step back they took toward the water drum.

Also in the kitchen were different containers of raw Kerala spices on a rickety spice table. The flat, hard, and heavy chevron-shaped black grinding stone stood on the three-foot-high wall beside the washroom. Its mate was the black rolling stone. I could gauge the condition of Ma's kitchen by checking out the grinding stones. The balder they were, the closer it was to a stone dresser's visit. Beads of sweat broke out above her upper lip as she struggled with their ineffectiveness and worked the spices to a fine paste needed for her great curries. Finally, the day arrived when Ma quit and called in the stone dresser to practice his art. After settling on a price, he chiseled the stones with thin horizontal friction lines. I watched the action as I sat opposite him, eyes scrunched for protection like a cat basking in the sunlight. I often felt the sting of the flying stone splinters on my face and knees while he casually went about his business, oblivious of the winged debris striking his unprotected face.

Dad entertained us in the evenings whenever the need arose. Dad constantly battled Deshmukh, the long-eared neighbor with the white caste threads hanging around his person, about his *langots* (loincloths). He sported ears so long and ugly that even a mosquito would have had second thoughts singing to him. Dad's show got going if he had to duck under the Deshmukh family heirlooms—those unsightly mile-long one-piece loincloths—to get into number 24 through the kitchen entrance. Mr. Deshmukh and his sons had their urine-stained loincloths washed and hung outside our door. Our families were not on speaking terms because of said loincloths. Dad, fuming, knocked on Deshmukh's door with the long-handled broom we used to remove cobwebs on our ceiling. Dad explained to Deshmukh that he should not exhibit his loincloths in full view of the women and children, reminded him that cleanliness is next to godliness, and asked when he would learn to be mindful.

"Mr. Deshmukh, you do not have the right to obstruct my entrance with your langots and invade my airspace. No one on this floor behaves in the manner you do. I am telling you, Mr. Deshmukh, remove your loincloths from my doorway before I do. Right... bloody... now."

As privileged as they come, Deshmukh never lifted a finger to comply. Dad took quick action. He picked them off with the broom and flung them at Deshmukh's door. Calling Dad a bloody fool, hurling expletives at us at will, the Brahmin was a spectacle to watch with the family's soggy heirlooms hanging around his neck, ear lobes bobbing. Dad entered the kitchen after quickly dispatching the loincloths, adjusting his glasses dangling on the tip of his nose. He pounded the ceiling with the broomstick, took several curtain calls, and declared he had won another battle, and the latest one was history. Dad solved a problem while teaching us basic hygiene and mindfulness.

In addition to lessons at home, Dad lived politics, breathed it, and passed it on to us. Dad believed Nehru should never have been India's first prime minister, although Gandhi favored him over others more capable, like Vallabhai Patel, the Iron Man, and Acharya Kripalani. Patel and Kripalani folded like accordions, fearing Gandhi; Kripalani withdrew his name before the selection, and Patel followed suit, although everyone except Gandhi supported him. Nehru was a pukka Harrow-schooled Brahmin aristocrat as stiff and upper-lipped as the last Viceroy of India, Earl Louis Mountbatten. According to Dad, he had no idea about the needs of ordinary Indians. Although Nehru may have resisted Partition, he buckled under pressure from the British and Jinnah (Gandhi's first choice of Prime Minister in undivided India and later Pakistan's heir apparent). There was a possibility that we could have avoided Partition and, therefore, its horrific aftermath. The estimated number of deaths due to Partition was between several hundred thousand and two million. Dad derided Nehru's much-heralded five-year plans. In his letters to the Times, Dad expressed his misgivings. Dad jested at the hollowness of the Hindi-Chini Bhai-Bhai slogan Nehru coined by calling Indians and Chinese brothers. In 1962, our Chinese 'brothers' engaged in a one-month border war over territory that is still unresolved. Then there was Nehru's masterpiece called '*Panchsheel*,' advertised then as his 'Five Principles of Peaceful Coexistence,' which, according to historians, was the brainchild of the Chinese Premier Chou En-Lai. Even though the all-powerful war-mongering Chairman Mao Tse-tung disowned his premier's idea, Nehru ran with it. Embarrassingly, Panchsheel lost its wheels after he sought 'Umbrella' protection from the US during the unprovoked Chinese incursions in 1962, engineered by Chairman Mao. Calling to intercede at the first sign of trouble contradicted his slogan and the Panchsheel he championed. Nehru died a broken man in 1964, never having thought the peace-loving Chou En-Lai would betray him, although perhaps Mao was to blame.

Even John wrote letters to the Times in addition to writing short stories. After the Cuban Missile Crisis, often cited as America's victory against the Soviets, he penned a letter to the Times. He pointed out that the Soviet Union removed the missiles only after America agreed they would never again invade Cuba, precisely what Cuba and the Soviets wanted.

———◆———

DAD TRIED HIS HAND at two businesses to make ends meet. His school textbook business, before my time, failed. He headed a small chit-fund company with his office friend, Mr. Joseph Sequiera, from our front room. Sequiera often talked to me before and after their meetings. Sequiera owned a Ford Prefect, and the fact that he could drive impressed me. While others, namely Sawant and the doctor downstairs, owned vehicles, they did not know how to drive and employed chauffeurs. Once the chit-fund meeting got underway, I watched them through my peephole. They were all crashing bores, including Dad, and I soon fell asleep hearing their babble. When it too failed, I inherited Dad's ledger books, which I used for many years as my cricket albums.

———◆———

IN 1987, ON A WORK trip to New York, I visited my niece. She surprised me with, "Mathew, everything in this house belongs to you." Perhaps rehearsed, she delivered it as if I were still that child. After working in a neighboring state, she married, and moved to New York. Inviting me was her first step toward reconciliation. Ma considered it heartfelt even three decades later: Ma was unsurprised by the invite; it was an old movie stirring up.

As an older matriculate, older than John, she lived with us for over a year. She quoted scripture like an automaton and made twelve-year-old me feel like a real low-life.

Eldest in her Brethren family of five children, she finally defied her father, who considered nursing demeaning. After failing to land a typist's job, she started RN training. Her old man did not speak to her for a year. With that RN degree, owing to my parents, she pulled it off–sponsored her four siblings, two boys and two girls, and their spouses to the US. Surprise, surprise—her sisters remained un-RNs. Stupidity even pays.

I met her three children. The two younger teenagers checked me out, and my reading came in handy. We discussed the origin of religion, as seen in "The Power of Myth," a series of public television interviews conducted by Rev. Bill Moyers with Dr. Joseph Campbell. We talked about other stuff too, and my niece was beside herself, making snide comments, calling Darwin and Campbell the devils, and naming me the 'enemy of the Bible.' I loved teaching moments like these. Heck, somebody had to disrupt and sow the seeds of inquiry and curiosity. Ironically but not surprisingly, I realized she'd done a volte-face on me the same evening she bequeathed me 'everything.' Hmm.

TOGETHER, DAD AND MA occupied a special place in my heart. Even though he failed in business, they carried on happily with the business of saving lives. Together, they did what was right regardless of hardship to help those who cried out to them. Besides providing much-needed comic relief, their actions helped build my resilience, self-confidence, and sense of humor. Although they deserved better, they were satisfied to see the fruits of their sacrifice in their children and those they helped.

Chapter 5: Montessori and Pigtails

At three and a half, I started Montessori. My two years there were a busy time with kids my age. On my first day, and so many like it, I dressed up as fast as I could, 'holing' all the buttons on my fly and shirt and buckling my sandals as Ma hurried me. All I knew about Montessori was that it would be my first school, and I loved its sound. As I proudly stressed the 'ss' sound, I said the word repeatedly while Ma and her friend looked on and smiled. The first time I walked to school with Ma, her friend, and Narayan behind us, ruffling my hair, I realized I was now part of the strange and exciting world I viewed from my windows.

"He has never been so excited. He says Montessori so clearly," Ma gushed to her friend, who was familiar with the Montessori and was accompanying us on my first day.

The school was within walking distance of home. It was a two-story building with a quaint green roof and a small, well-flowered compound. There was plenty of playtime and tinkering, along with learning the ABCs and numbers, one, two, and three to ten. Inside were many pretty girls with pigtails and tiny spots of black kohl eyeliner on their flushed cheeks to ward off the evil eye and a generous amount on their eyelids to make them prettier than they already were. I wondered why they could not use the same bathroom as the boys. After all, I knew of no problems my mother and sister had with our bogs.

Rabindranath Tagore, an Indian polymath, knew of Madame Montessori's early learning methods and established Tagore-Montessori schools as early as 1929. The pioneering Italian woman and her son arrived in India in 1939 to establish a

Montessori teacher-training center. Once India entered WW II in 1940, the British labeled the Italians 'enemy aliens' and canceled the Montessoris' return home. They stayed on after the war and left India only in 1947.

Narayan dropped me off in the mornings, and we meandered back home in the afternoons, taking in the sights. Upon Ma's insistence, he brought my hat, and I was the only child in the neighborhood who wore a western hat to ward off the searing mid-afternoon sun. Thanks, Ma. The narrow sidewalks were a mixed bag—pedestrians in a hurry competing with shoppers who moved slowly. As a pedestrian, I could see why it was tempting to jaywalk, and Narayan ensured I didn't get tempted. Screeching brakes and uninterrupted honking ruled the road as vehicular traffic trod carefully since street justice was always ready for instant delivery by our intrepid pedestrians as they sidestepped onto the street at will.

The imposing Ranjit Film Studio, an impregnable fortress with its ten-foot concrete wall crowned with glass shards, stood across the street from the Montessori. Heading home, the studio was Narayan's favorite time-wasting stop. Ma sent him to the movies occasionally, and he was sure to be star-struck. Like Narayan, the crowds gathered around the gate to catch a glimpse of their heartthrobs. Sometimes, the studio bosses called them in as extras. The *chaukidar* (gatekeeper) was in charge of the enormous steel gate to the studio. The stars arrived in their fancy, foreign luxury vehicles, wearing flashy sunglasses to the roaring approval of the crowd. The gatekeeper would emerge from his shack with his hands in the namaskar position, smiling and greeting them respectfully.

One of the few times it made it worthwhile was during my senior year at Montessori when we gathered outside the studio gate along with the big crowd. A well-known actor and his entourage were waiting at the entrance. I could not see or hear anything being the shortest. There was no chance that the crowd, buzzing with expectations of what was to come, would let us squeeze our way to the front. I clamored for Narayan to carry me. He reluctantly heaved me off my feet and put me on his shoulders. I was now the tallest of the lot with an unsurpassed view. It was like window-watching with binoculars. Combined with their gestures, expressions, and words, I had picked here and there, I followed the unfolding drama.

The gatekeeper was a big, well-built fellow. None too impressed by the gatekeeper's warm welcome, the young chauffeur insulted the older fellow by saying, "Enough, enough of this *swagatam* [welcome]. Last time, we told you always to leave the gate open for us. Hurry up, chaukidar. I have to drive the sahib next to Chembur studio, understand?"

The gatekeeper shrugged his shoulders, implying that whether he drove or crawled was not his concern. Although a bit ruffled, he gave them a respectful nod.

"I can't do that, driver. There's always a crowd at the gate, and the sahib ordered the gates to remain locked. If you have a problem, please speak with the sahib, not me. I'm only his peon," he said, smiling and exhibiting his betel-stained teeth.

"Okay... open the damn gate. Keep the lecture to yourself. Don't stand there like a *gadha* [donkey]."

The fellow craned out the window and spat the betel and areca dregs. The red spittle streaked a line close to where the gatekeeper stood. He was earnestly seeking a confrontation with the genial gatekeeper for no reason. This petulance and showmanship by the driver were unnecessary. With fists jammed into his pockets, the gatekeeper was the picture of controlled anger.

"Now, what did you say? I didn't hear you."

"*Aré Ullu ka patta* [Hey son-of-an-owl or fool], you heard me."

Calling him a fool made it worse.

"Can you say it louder so that all these good people clamoring to see the sahib and his sahiba can hear what I have to put up with? Also, it is better to talk to your elders respectfully."

The gatekeeper stood near the automobile, fists still smoldering in his pockets. Realizing that this back-and-forth was getting him no closer to his movie set, the actor decided to play peacemaker. He rolled down his window and pleaded with the gatekeeper.

"Listen, *bhai* [brother], my driver is a fool. I agree he is an upstart and does not respect his elders. I will take care of that. Please open the gate, and here's something for you," the actor said, extending his hand with a rupee note. Startled, the gatekeeper's face turned red. The actor could not have known that my gatekeeper had top billing for the show today. Respectfully bringing his hands together in a namaskar, the chaukidar said, "No, sir, please keep the *chai-pani* [bribe], sir. Please ask your driver to show some respect for us, the less fortunate. We are not dogs to be kicked around by this city boy."

His genuine plea got a sigh from all the spectators and got us all rooting for him. He strolled deliberately, one meditative step at a time, and unlocked the gate. After that, he stood there with the padlock in his hand. He was in no mood to extend his usual courtesy of swinging open the gate. The actor and his entourage were ready to take matters into their own hands. The only things that kept them from beating the gatekeeper were his physique, the padlock he held, and the crowds at the gate. Not to mention that these actors and their lackeys were usually nothing more than talk, which is all they did anyway.

With one wary eye on the gatekeeper, the driver crouched, slithering alongside the vehicle, reaching the gate. Sliding the latch, he inched the gate open. The crowd pressed forward, ready to deliver some home-brewed justice. They stopped short when the gatekeeper gave the travelers a brisk salute, waving them into the studio. As the entourage moved on, I saw the actor gesticulating and shouting at his driver. He was one teed-off idol. The chaukidar shut the gate, locked it, and went to his shack with a wide grin and a nod to us all.

The crowd was speechless until one of them spoke for all of us, "Oh man. What a dialogue! What acting! We have never seen the old man like this."

The people I crossed paths with—some heroes, many zeroes, and others simply a mix—made up my world. They lived fighting, winning, and losing, but never giving up. Human emotion and qualities — anger, joy, grit, sadness, and caring—were different sides of the dice. What mattered most was mixing these in the right proportions and mutual respect. With his audacity, the humble gatekeeper was the able-bodied version of my Otta Kaiyan. He was the silent assassin—deadly, lethal. Star struck as Narayan was with the 'talced' characters of the silver screen, not one of them could hold a candle to my genial gatekeeper.

Rules mattered. So did spurning enticement and standing your ground. After learning these lessons, I had to keep tugging Narayan to meander our way back home to Ma. I was sure Ma was worried sick, I told myself.

Life lessons were piling around me everywhere, including my home, pleading for attention. Like the Times of India's famous cartoonist, R.K. Laxman's iconic, simple-looking commoner, I was an observant sponge. I hoped someday to be as wise as he was.

Chapter 6: Now for the Big School

Next, I entered the big stage—John's school—and started in pre-primary, becoming a 'lifer' at Dr. Antonio DaSilva High School, a Catholic school in West Dadar, established in 1858. The three of us went to school together that year. The following year, John joined college, and Elisabeth led the formation of two.

We crossed the footbridge over the railway lines, which connected East and West Dadar on the way to school. One of three streets that led from the roundabout in front of my school was the quarter-mile road from the footbridge; the second led south to Elisabeth's Convent Girls High School, half a mile south of my school, and the third went north to Tilak Bridge. The roundabout had three quadrants: a small Hindu temple, a Christian cross, and a traffic police enclosure. Close by was a mosque. The commotion of the big school and its surroundings had sounds of its own, imagined and palpable, that echoed in my ears. Over the silvery sound of children squealing and the gong-gong of the school bell, which rang every 40 minutes, I heard the traffic cop's shrill whistles and the jingle of the temple bells that the faithful rang, stirring up the gods despite the *pujari* (Hindu priest) having already done so with his droning incantations. Cupping my ears, I could sometimes luckily make out the muezzin's faint calls from atop the mosque's minaret, beseeching the faithful to prayer.

On the way home, there was much to do, see, and hear. On the road to the footbridge was the *Kabutar Khana* (Pigeon House) roundabout, where countless pigeons dined all day. I watched the pigeons—standard gray ones, white ones, and rare reddish-brown ones—jostle and gurgle their way to the best spots. Next, I sometimes walked through the long, winding department store enclave, stopped at many stores, and ogled stuff I would one day have. After all the sightseeing, I headed home on the busy bridge, populated by hawkers selling trinkets and hustlers who enticed unwitting pedestrians into impromptu betting and card-guessing games, relieving them of their hard-earned wages.

In the early months of the big school, I had a memorable face-off with John. I sometimes helped Dad with his cufflinks while he had breakfast, and John got after me if I ended up with different ones on each cuff.

"What did I tell you? The idiot has done it again," jeered John. He would then bring up my most embarrassing mistakes and keep at them until I lost my cool. I chased him with anything I could grab. I would launch my so-called 'missiles,' one after the other, as he escaped to the kitchen and banged shut the doors on me. As I threw the missiles over the kitchen doorjamb, I was too young to know all he had to do to avoid them was to remain flat against the doors—a Physics law about projectiles, I learned years later!

One time, when he hid behind the kitchen door, I bolted out of our front door with a 'missile' in hand, sped around both verandas, and screeched to a stop at our back door as I listened, short of breath, heart a-pumping wildly, and ears throbbing against the kitchen door. I brushed the 'missile' on the wall and lit the fuse, as cowboys do when they light cigarettes. The rustling leaves of the jambool tree, standing behind the building with its canopy shrouding the open sky behind the bogs, stirred a whiff that nearly overpowered me. It was no time to walk away from a mere irritant to my olfactory senses. I could hear the 'famous one' asking Ma what was taking the idiot so long—I held my ear to the doors again—and with a magician's flourish—I pushed them wide open.

"Yeshu Christu," I gasped, imitating Ma. He was scared stiff, splayed against the doors, eyes pinched shut, hands outstretched like a crucifix, transfixed. The way he stood flattened against the doors, every single one of my projectiles was a stunningly harmless dud. Yet, he appeared shaken.

I had my first triumph over my brother. When he opened his eyes, he realized two universal truths. He was a giant squid—and I was no idiot. He grasped another fact—I did not intend to hurt him. I held John's hockey ball securely in my hand. I finally discovered one of the ways to handle a tormenter and emerge victorious.

I was always looking for their acceptance. Yeah, that's right; it was the one thing my siblings had over me. Although all the 'forgiving' I did only encouraged the two, it kept the peace. Like a shock absorber with memory, not forgetting was the result. I could have fallen through the cracks due to their bullying, but for my rock, my caring parents. Ma and Dad may have told my siblings to knock it off, but I'm not entirely sure, since the two never quit, to this day, although I gave up holding my breath. My lack of whining and crying made them think I had a sterner backbone, which couldn't have been farther from the truth.

⎯⎯⎯◉⎯⎯⎯

DIRECTLY BELOW OUR north-facing bedroom window was the restaurant terrace, where the servers, cooks, and kitchen help slept at night on their hammock-like *charpoys* (coir cots). During my morning watch, I became aware of a character called Mohammed and his daily antics. Unlike the other workers, Mohammed usually overslept, had his sheet pulled over his head, and lay there immovable like a starfish.

Usually, one of his calm, patient coworkers, whom I nicknamed the *Imam* (the person who leads prayers in a mosque), came to wake him. At first, the calm Imam cajoled Mohammed into waking up, and it got progressively testier. The Imam finally shed his peaceful garb and swore at him, invoking his parents, and when that did not work, he kicked the charpoy in exasperation, followed by more cursing. Taking hold of Mohammed's shoulders, the Imam shook him violently. Mohammed reacted with a blast of bad words and dared the Imam to touch him again as he continued to sleep. Finally, the Imam shuffled away noisily to complain to the owner. Mohammed buckled and followed him, rubbing his eyes sheepishly, muttering.

I was rooting for the Imam. Mohammed also needed a lecture about delaying me. 'Come on, Mohammed,' I invariably screamed, 'the same show every day? When will you grow up, you lazy bum? You have to wake up, so why not get up on time? You make me late every time you pull this stunt.' I don't think he cared to listen to my shouting. In work, as in play, timeliness was everything. As you can see, between Otta Kaiyan, Sawant sahib, and the minions, Deshmukh, Mohammed, and my Imam, I received free tutorials in salty Hindi, Urdu, and Marathi, perhaps even before I had mastered my numerals and alphabet.

———●———

IN 1956, THOUSANDS of outcastes from around the Bombay metropolis came to Main Road, where the outcaste millworkers and their families lived, and marched peacefully. It was a moving experience as I watched them and heard their mournful chant, which went on for days: *'sangham saranam gachhami, dharmam saranam gachhami, budham saranam gachhami,'* which translates to 'I take refuge in the sangha (the community), I take refuge in the dharma (law of nature), I take refuge in Budha.' I learned that their illustrious outcaste leader, Dr. Bhimrao Ambedkar, had passed away. He left Hinduism 20 years earlier but did not renounce it until October 1956, when he became a Buddhist. He died that December. Years later, I realized I had watched history in the making. Bhimrao was born an outcaste and was the subject of the most inhumane treatment by higher-caste Hindus throughout his childhood and adulthood. They forced him to sit outside the classroom door rather than inside during school. 'Outclassed' indeed. Bhimrao suffered but never broke under Hinduism's heavy yoke. Undaunted, he withstood all of it and had a life filled with prodigious achievements. He became an eminent jurist, an economist, and a social scholar.

His economic writings focused on the intersection of race, caste, and class differences. He coined the word *Dalit* (broken people) for his lot because the caste system had 'broken' them and preordained their fate even before their birth. As the architect of the Constitution of India, he ensured Dalits had a voice in free India. He fought for their emancipation from the different forms of casteism that thrived in India. Hinduism had failed him, and his fellow Dalits converted to Buddhism en masse—in the millions—all over India. Although millions left Hinduism, its chokehold did not leave them, and their plight did not change overnight. The struggle for equality continues in India and other parts of the world. Still.

'Caste' by Isabel Wilkerson discusses the prevalence of caste throughout world history. She says color is a fact, and race is a social construct. I might further expound that the dark melanin in skin tone has evolved to protect people from the Sun's UV rays; thus, people closer to the equator, where the Sun's rays are more direct, tend to have darker skin. A fellow traveler and I stumbled into Darwin's Theory. She, like me, believed in evolution, but its sheer extent surprised her when I said long, slender noses (like hers) were also a tiny part of said theory; she rejoined, "How so?" I explained how nostrils condition air, and longer noses warm the cold air slightly longer in colder climates, providing protection from infections. I could have pointed out the evolutionary reasons for eye coloration for emphasis. Then, I was not on a lecture tour; I was just a fellow wayfarer.

THE LUXURY ARAM COURT apartments stood diagonally opposite Sabita building. Three stores were on the ground floor of Aram Court. The first was a Malayali-owned coffee and tea store, and the second was a Parsi-owned liquor store. Prohibition was in full force except for expat foreigners and important-looking Indians who frequented the liquor store. They arrived in their chauffeur-driven vehicles, made purchases, and then escaped to their luxurious homes in places like Malabar Hill or Peddar Road. I watched in amusement as they held their noses to escape the rancid smell of the rotting trash the street cleaners piled at the storefront for collection. They rushed out quickly with their helpers, with wicker baskets of the best brews I was sure I would never taste.

The large English movie billboards for movie theaters in downtown Bombay were between the stores' outside walls. These ads targeted the patrons of the liquor store. We read these too, believe me —especially my big brother. Cinemas in downtown Bombay often changed shows on Fridays. Usually, on Thursdays, they replaced the billboards. My highlight of Thursday afternoon was seeing what new movies were coming to town. We saw 'Seven Brides for Seven Brothers' upon his recommendation. Therefore, I could assume I would see some of the advertised movies. The subsequent movie endorsement from the famous one, which Dad and Ma went to, was an adult movie called 'I'll Cry Tomorrow' with Susan Hayward. Elisabeth and I stayed home for that one. After the all-knowing one endorsed it, Dad and Elisabeth went to see Rock Around the Clock. It left me out again. He said there was too much scandalous stuff—like kissing and whatnot—between boys and girls. Besides, 'Oh, was I not too young for that... blah... blah... blah... blah. I had Ma all to myself that evening; she entertained me and soothed hurt feelings by letting me help her cook. John, the dialogue and plot explainer-in-chief, went with the tribe to all the movies and regularly saw them again with his friends.

In the late afternoons, the Municipal workers, outcaste Hindus called *Bhangis*, collected the refuse around the stores and the billboards. They dragged all the black, coagulated trash in wicker baskets to the large pile near the liquor store. Lower than the lowest in the rigid four-tiered Hindu *Varna* or caste system, the untouchables—who Gandhiji lovingly called *Harijan* or children of the Hindu God Vishnu —did this work daily. Soon, even Gandhi's well-meaning Harijan became a slur for casteless people, the same as an outcaste, untouchable, or *Achūta* (one born condemned without the possibility of rebirth). Flipping names without improving their condition was useless. I am sure Gandhi knew better. Calling them Dalit (broken people) was more honest.

The basis of the caste system per Manu's Laws buried in the Hindu texts likens the system to the functioning of the human body. First, in my thinking, missing from Manu's 'manifesto'—not even deigned a mention—what lay beneath the feet in the dirt: the outcasts, the oppressed—serving out their karma based on their past misdeeds.

The four castes mentioned by Manu were the Shudras–the feet–the toilers; the Vaishyas–the thighs–the engine–the tradesmen; the Kshatriyas–the arms–the protectors and rulers; the Brahmins–the head, the mouth, the sage—nearest to the gods.

Forgotten or missing among Manu's self-serving laws was this fact. Along with the ground, the body walked on, each of the interdependent body parts mentioned would fail catastrophically with the absence of any one of them.

Years later, I learned how bad it was for the outcastes. Just like mighty elephants still felt chained even though only a light rope existed where before they dragged a heavy chain, so were the outcastes —conditioned to an invisible fate for life, never to be around or heard. Even their shadows were polluting. The outcastes accepted their preordained destiny and had no way out of it. You know they had taken this divine decree as the truth when you saw their half-naked, rickets-ridden children playing in the mire close to them. The caste system ensured that these children never saw a book or a piece of paper and pencil, let alone step into a schoolroom. I wondered aloud whether they should not be the highest-paid people in the world. My all-knowing brother scoffed.

"They are just Bhangis, Mathew, and that's all they know and want to do. They are lazy illiterates, you understand. Pay them the highest! Even Gandhi would have trouble figuring you out."

He made sure everyone around knew the extent of my idiocy.

Can you believe this? Two boys from the same home, ten years apart—how it all whizzed by his cerebrum faster than light! They say the oldest one is always the most intelligent of the rest. Is that so? Four years of that one-on-one treatment, no, make it ten, being the only boy until I showed up, did not do him any favors in a patriarchal community. Maybe that is where he got his little emperor complex —no sharing or caring. No daring either—not bold enough to empathize with the Bhangis, given the stark contrasts we breathed, lived, and saw daily. Maybe hanging Napoleon's picture at his desk was the extent of his daring. Many years later, my doubts became clearer. He was not protecting me for the future. He was inoculating himself from relatives who came through our tenement, my fellow downtrodden Indians, and above all, our family.

As I watched them clearing the rubbish barefoot, ill equipped, ankle-deep in the primordial ooze, bent but unbroken, with nothing but brooms and weeping bamboo wicker baskets, I felt sad, helpless, and weepy. It seemed only fair to pay them the highest wages. Why not? That was who I was. Sorry, I am. That is what Dad and Ma had taught me.

Such was my father's house in our lovely 'well-fenestrated' tenement. Even as life lessons piled up during those penury-filled years, as such, situations often do, they were the happiest times of my life, as such circumstances sometimes are.

CHAPTER 6 PICTURES:

1. Big school play: I am the second person from the right in the back row.
2. Big school: (two front views, photos 2023)
3. Big school traffic roundabout in front of my school, photo 2023.

Chapter 7: Pigeons' Revenge

My best friend Chinka lived on our floor at number 18. Like Dickens's Tiny Tim, he was a sickly fellow. His parents were Hindus from the neighboring state of Gujarat. His stern, mysterious-looking father always wore semi-dark glasses and rarely spoke or smiled. Chinka's mother, Ma's good friend, was a thin, shriveled, gentle, taciturn woman with a bent back, a large hooked nose, and an irritating nasal tone. : Another woman, quite pretty, plucky, and younger than Chinka's mom, also lived there; whom Chinka called his second mom. His eldest brother, as emaciated-looking as his mother, was about the same age as John. The middle brother, who resembled Chinka's second mom, was a smart-looking, bespectacled high schooler and was as talkative as Chinka.

Chinka's west-side neighbors were the Muslims at number 17. The woman of the house was also Ma's friend. The smell of the meat they cooked was mouth-watering. During festivals like Ramzan or Bakr-Id, the kebab and biriyani smells wafted from their kitchen and infused the rest of the floor. It yawned all the way to the Daniel tenement at Bog's end. The fragrance was a welcome change and went on nightly for a whole month. During the festivities, clad in a head-to-toe burqa robe with a fancy crocheted window around her eyes, she dropped by with vermicelli *payasam*, a delectable, semi-solid, milk-based, ingredient-filled sweet dish. She never did bring mutton biriyani. I knew the meat dish's ambrosial smells were as close as I would ever get to the heaven of Mughlai delicacies.

Chinka's north-side neighbor in number 19 was Mr. Karmarkar, a widower with two children, Sulabha and Sharad. He remarried, and his second wife came straight out of stepmother school. Centrally cast in her archetypal role, she was mean, vindictive, and conniving. She could fool anyone with her niceness, which she often did. After completing her daily chores, including beating and berating Sulabha and Sharad, she was bored witless and usually sat on the front veranda, sifting her hair with a nit-comb. She decapitated most of the lice on the spot with her sharp nails and stamped out the scurrying ones on the floor with her slipper. Other times, she vacuously sat sharpening her claws. When Mr. Karmarkar came home, she gave him an earful of gossip and complained about his lazy children.

We played on the veranda, and I heard snippets of the Karmarkars squabbling. Mr. Karmarkar pestered her for tea, biscuits, and some loving care, like kneading his worn-out calves or scratching his back before hearing her out. She sat by his feet, pouting like a Hindi film vamp, and often told him she would not do any of it unless he first listened to her complaints. She grumbled most about Sharad. He ran errands up and down those three floors, constantly doing thankless chores for the stepmother and the Muslim neighbor. The Muslim woman rewarded him with tips, while all he got from his stepmother was her scorn. During these trips, he met Sawant sahib's hooligans and wasted hours hearing their captivating stories. The Sabita parents noticed this, so their children followed their warnings and avoided Sharad.

The Ijankars, Maharashtrian Hindus, lived next door to Karmarkar at number 20. Mr. Ijankar's first wife died before my time, and he had two grown sons from his first marriage and two children (Vijaya and Deepak) from his second wife, Prema. Ma's best friend, Prema, was her eyes and ears. She kept a wary eye on me when Sharad and I played, and we lived four doors away from them. She came home to see Ma in the afternoons and gossiped while I slept. After shopping, Ma often stopped by Prema's door by the stairs and visited her.

When Sharad was not around, Vijaya would join Chinka and me in our hide-and-seek games. She sometimes brought Kamala, Sawant sahib's daughter, to play with us; it was more fun when Kamala joined us. She was the oldest, a bit bossy, and set the rules, so we all got equal turns as the police or thieves. Her natural porcelain beauty and wavy, jet-black hair, which outlined her pretty face, struck me. A tiny spot of kohl on her cheek warded off the evil eye. I liked her well-fitting pastel dresses, prim and proper, adorned with matching lace at the hemline. In short, she was classy, unlike Vijaya, who was like one of us urchins.

Chinka's mother allowed him to play only on our floor. Sharad and I took advantage of this fact once and ended up on the ground floor, leaving Chinka searching uselessly for us. We surreptitiously searched for cigarette butts on the Sabita driveway. Sharad picked them up and stuffed them into his pockets, and I did the same. The longer the butts, the luckier we felt. I knew we would soon be smoking these. The where, how, and when of smoking these remained a mystery and left me confused and scared, with a tinge of guilt as I wondered whether this would meet Ma's approval. With my pockets bulging with cigarette butts, I followed Sharad upstairs to the tall electrical junction box on our floor, next to Sharad's tenement. The gap between the junction box ledge and the ceiling allowed for a perfect nesting spot for some gray pigeons. I kept a few long butts and gave the remaining to Sharad. He climbed the steel tubes carrying the electrical wires and hid most of our cache near the pigeons' nests. My admiration for him grew with every perilous step he took toward the top of the junction box. Concerned by the invasion, the pigeons issued warning gurgles before they flew off. They perched close by, bobbing their heads, peering to see what Sharad was doing. The gurgling reached a fever pitch each time he moved, dropping to a low murmur when they watched his harmless actions. Our summer of fun and smoking was ahead of schedule.

Finally, as Sharad clambered down, nailing his final acrobatic leap for a neat floor landing, his stepmother appeared out of nowhere.

"What are you doing?" she demanded and gave him a whack across the back of his head, which caused Sharad to lurch forward and run headlong into me. I rocked like a pinball before I fell. I quickly staggered back up. Sharad regained his equilibrium and stood there unflinching. She swung another with her other hand, and I realized she was viciously ambidextrous. Sharad, though hurt, refused to cry, which made her furious. Finally, she flashed her gaze towards me and attacked me, "Unlike your useless self, Sharad has work to do. I heard your mother does everything for you. Is that right?" she asked me, one eyebrow raised over her narrowed eye. I started a conversation with the lunatic so Sharad could escape her.

"I have the best mother in the world, way smarter than you. Have you seen her pretty hair? It is longer than yours, and it reaches her knees. She is prettier than you and loves me more, too."

"Wait till I see your mother. Calling me ugly of all things, you little nitwit."

"Auntie, I said Ma's just prettier."

I saw Sharad turn around to beckon me before vanishing into the bogs. I ran to the bogs and disappeared before Sharad's stepmother could engage me more with her useless tit-for-tat. I now knew the 'where,' but I feared the bogs more than anything.

Sharad signaled me to come to the last stall, finger on his lips, miming that someone was in the adjacent booth. Curious and afraid, I entered the enclosure, and Sharad latched the door behind me. I shuddered at the sight of the dreaded keyhole.

He lit two butts like a pro and handed me one of them, and without a word spoken, I watched spellbound as he put on an excellent demonstration of a smoker's repertoire of tricks, making rings and blowing smoke through his nostrils. I inhaled and choked immediately. The smoke went to my sphincter, and I felt it constrict. Before I could emulate him, I had the most untimely coughing fit, and suddenly, Sharad started giggling.

I heard sounds of annoyance coming from the next stall, followed by a swish of water, the unlatching of the door, and a quick shuffle out of the booth. Meanwhile, I tried to emulate the maestro through the blinding smoke, and I soon inhaled and exhaled with ease despite the annoying coughing spells. Soon, Sharad threw all his spent butts into the keyhole, and I walked right up to my phobia, stared at it without flinching, and did likewise. Crouching out of the bogs, I looked left and immediately locked eyes with Prema, standing at her doorway as she sneered disapprovingly. I was sure she was the occupant of the stall next to ours. The nasty cigarette taste stayed in my mouth, and every breath now reminded me of Prema's sneer. I ran to my tenement, all torn up inside, as my thoughts of being another deadbeat like Sharad chased me. I fell into our steel bed and pretended to sleep—the where, when, and how no longer mattered.

Ma was making tea when I heard a knock on the door, and there was Prema, the woman who never quit. I was the main topic of their chat.

'Don't you have better things to do than to tattle to Ma? Why not talk to Mrs. Karmarkar about Sharad and see if she cares?'

I did not care to hear anymore. Ma reminded Prema to keep it low, which helped me finally doze off. I was soon dreaming, and in my dream, someone like Ma tried to do a 'Mohammed' on me. I wanted to ask, 'Can't you see Ma that I am not Mohammed?' but no words came out, and I couldn't distinguish between their faces as Prema continued to whisper intently to Ma while they moved out of earshot.

My hungry self woke up to the enticing smells of food from the kitchen. Finally, Ma came smiling with a tumbler of tea and a plate of hot, deep-fried lentil fritters with coconut chutney. I kept wondering what had transpired between Prema and Ma. Maybe Prema confessed to Ma that she had not seen me smoking. There was no chance that Ma had forgotten the darned incident while she was busy in the kitchen.

I had tea and waited for the fritters to cool down. Ma blew on the first one and then bit into it to let the steam out. She dipped it in the coconut chutney and fed me. I ate a few more, a chutney dip preceding each bite. Although the snacks and tea filled me up, they could not mask the taste of the cigarette in my mouth. Ma smiled when I rubbed my tummy, and soon saw her eyes well up. I asked Ma what the matter was with her.

"I don't want to lose you, my precious son."

I reminded her I was not lost and was right in front of her. Ma stared right through me with her teary eyes.

"Prema said you and Sharad were giggling and coughing next to her stall, and she sure smelled cigarette smoke."

"Ma, I wasn't even there. I played hide and seek with Chinka, and he ran home."

"Lying is bad, and lying to your Ma is even worse," she said, reaching for the newspaper.

"How do you know I was smoking, and how can you believe nosy Prema?"

"I believe her, and yes, you came in smelling like a cigarette. She worries about you the way I do."

"Oh, Ma," I cried when I fended off the first whack of the rolled-up newspaper with my arm. That stung, and I got off the bed. The second one landed on my derrière, and that stung even more.

"The first one is for lying, the second one for smoking, and this one for calling Prema nosy," as she gave me another whack. I could not believe Ma had whacked me. However, she had been careful to use a newspaper instead of going bonkers like Sharad's stepmother. I ran right into Ma before she could get in another whack. With my hands around her legs, I burrowed my face in the sari's folds like a whimpering newborn marsupial. With firm finality, she had me promise I would never play with Sharad again. That is the end, I thought.

"Let's go to Chinka's place," Ma said.

I was reeking with shame as we proceeded to number 18. I did not know how to convince Ma I was not a lying, cigarette-smoking scoundrel.

Chinka's mother welcomed us in, and he was fast asleep. He stirred around and was surprised to see so many eyeballs staring at him. He panicked for a second and then relaxed when he realized one of those pairs was mine.

"Hey, Mathew?" he asked, rubbing his eyes. "I searched for you everywhere."

"Oh? Where?" I asked him in amazement.

"You vanished," his mother interrupted.

Turning towards Ma, she stated the facts.

"One minute, they were playing. Then Chinka came home crying, convinced someone had kidnapped his best friend."

I reminded her I was with Sharad the whole time.

"He was with Sharad all right," Ma chimed. "Prema found them loitering around."

We left Chinka's tenement as the mothers continued chatting about the families. We planted ourselves close to the electrical box, and Sharad's door was ominously ajar. Ma seemed in no hurry as I tugged her toward number 24. The pigeons were too close for comfort, and so was Sharad's stepmother.

Mrs. Karmarkar poked her inquisitive head around her half-open door. With her nit-comb lodged on her head, she smiled devilishly at us, staring Ma up and down. She burst out laughing.

"You know, Mrs. Daniel, your youngest is the smartest talker I have ever met."

I was flabbergasted and waited for more.

Ma ruffled my head with some pride, taken aback, as she blushed. Sharad's stepmom was being as pleasant as possible; perhaps Ma was relishing it like the first Alphonso mango of the season. The named mango cultivar, with a Portuguese name, is a world-renowned variety that's grown in Ratnagiri, Maharashtra.

Regaining her composure, Ma asked. "Oh, what did he say?"

"We were just talking. Oh, look at your beautiful black hair," Sharad's stepmother continued, "It's such a blessing to have hair so long like your boy was telling me."

Mrs. Karmarkar stepped towards me, all smiles, and ruffled my hair. Soon, she dug her sharp nail into my scalp and followed it up with another. She dared me to scream as I doubled over in pain.

Ma had just heard Mrs. Karmarkar praise us both. Ma had heard about this woman from Prema and Mrs. Salvi, the dentist's wife, but she wasn't known for bestowing compliments. I could have ended the meeting had I only screamed in pain and told her that the witch had nailed me twice.

The pigeons were having a gurgling competition, annoyed with all the commotion below their lair, even as I tugged Ma. I heard a flutter of wings as more pigeons glided back in and settled down. The gurgling intensified, and then a cigarette butt hit the floor. Fresh encounters with a rolled-up newspaper seemed likely as a shower of cigarette butts followed. It got everyone's attention as we all looked up. Coming clean crossed my mind, but it was too late. The pigeons decided to clean their stinking quarters in solidarity with Ma's anti-smoking campaign.

"What's going on?" Mrs. Karmarkar exclaimed. "Do pigeons use cigarette butts for their nests?"

"They use anything, according to my big brother," I volunteered.

I knew she liked my little gem, and I ducked in time when she reached for my scalp.

"Oh, is that so? I think the Sabita pigeons have started smoking," my mother smoldered mockingly with a raised eyebrow and melted me with laser beams of pure light. With lips pursed together, she marched me back to number 24. Luckily, she did not reach for the newspaper.

Instead, she sat me down face-to-face and lectured me.

"Did you get all those cigarette butts from the filthy street?"

"Did you know that someone else had smoked them?"

"Did you know that people have germs in their spittle, which you inhale into your lungs that could make you sick?"

"Why didn't you play hide and seek? Why did you run from Chinka and go down to the street?"

"Why didn't you tell me anything?"

The questions kept coming, and I concluded that Ma was not looking for answers; she couldn't care less, as she went on rat-a-tat-tat like one of those fast and furious typists at the typing shop around the corner.

"You are going to wash your mouth with some potassium permanganate."

Her nurse training came in like eagles screeching in for a kill. She was ready to obliterate all the lurking germs, including Exhibit Number One—me. Thanks to my godmother, Matron Mary, we had a vial marked KMNO4.

"Then I will cleanse you with an oil bath," she added as a subscript.

She brought down the law on me with precision and clarity. I should clarify further—she meant the dreaded *Abhayangam*, the oil baths I hated with all my being.

Then the clincher – the super subscript – "Never play with Sharad again, dear. I will tell Dad everything."

As we dashed into the valley of mind games, I knew there was no stopping her. Dad would not even have to admonish me; his hurt look would do more than any wound-up newspaper ever could, which was the tactic Ma knew I feared most. She endearingly herded me to the washroom. I must say something about *kuzhambu* (the blended oil) used in the oil bath while I can still breathe. The oil has many ingredients, too many to mention. I think they ran out of herbs for this Ayurvedic cure-all. The base oils and powdered ingredients simmer for a while, and then the mixture undergoes a filtration process. The stuff is thick and sticky as honey. She stood me on the washroom parapet, and she peeled off my clothes, gagging overdramatically at the smoke smell on each. I was to undergo a full-body oil application and massage. The specially brewed oil would bring several health benefits, especially mental ones.

With hawk-like determination, she slapped it on and rubbed it into every pore with quiet authority, including under my crotch, armpits, and even soles. I wondered how layering my *pāda-mūlam* (soles of feet), described in Sanskrit literature, with *kuzhambu*, would save my smoking soul.

She used coconut oil on the scalp and face because kuzhambu is unsuitable for those areas. I burnished like a well-oiled *pahalwan* (Indian wrestler). My body glistened while all my pores screamed in protest. I felt the primeval ooze finally slithering through my cavities, my pores, and, I was sure, into my bloodstream.

After this, she set me on the kerosene can and left me languishing. More spankings would have been better than hanging around the washroom in the all-pervading smell. I did not realize that today's waiting included extra time for reflection. Ma was ready with her finale, and as she watered me down, she scrubbed me with a wad of *inja* known botanically as Acacia caesia, a medicinal tree-bark exfoliant. It was the most painful substitute for soap ever discovered. The inja absorbs most of the malodorous blended oil and leaves behind a pleasant smell. Ma scrubbed until my skin was on fire and ready to peel away. I understood why Ma came up with the idea of giving me an oil bath with all the scrubbing it entailed. Then she scrubbed my scalp with the inja.

"Ma, that hurts."

"What hurts?"

"My head, Ma, she dug her nail in twice."

"Who did?"

"Sharad's mother."

She separated my hair, felt the welts on my head, and gasped. Her eyes told me she was thinking hard, wondering how this was possible. Not believing me, she asked when it had happened, and I replied that she had done it when she reached and patted my head—another gasp.

"Right in front of you, Ma." She did not think anybody could be that brazen.

She bent over, kissed the welts, rinsed me off, wiped me clean, combed my hair, and watched me run to bed. I was half gone by now. Falling asleep, I thought Ma would not lose me to the Karmarkars or anyone else, not in a thousand years. She wiped off the sweat on her upper lip and lay down with her head next to mine, knowing her toils may have paid off.

Before falling asleep, I asked, "Ma, can you sing me the lullaby about the *kozhi* [hen]?"

Silence followed a muffled sob, and I realized that there were to be no lullabies. Finally overcome, I said, "I love you, Ma." I cuddled in her exhausted arms, and we both went to sleep.

When I woke up, instead of Ma, Dad was beside me, doubled over, reading a book. I stirred around, only to see Dad looking at me intently. His tummy felt cold as if he had just had his evening bath. Before he could say anything, I reached for the orb, its roundness. No longer could I resist rolling on it and lying face down. He smelled nice, baby talcum nice. I could feel his breathing as his chest heaved. Then he moved his stomach up and down slowly. He was playing the game we usually played when he lay down after his evening bath. He was the train driver, and I was the passenger. My head bobbed back and forth with the train's movement. I closed my eyes, looked out, and felt the train hurtling its way to Victoria Terminus (VT). The train was still moving as we took a flying leap off it like our brave Bombay commuters. We ran to the New Empire Restaurant opposite VT. The waiter took his time coming around. I ordered a plate of meat samosas for myself and Dad's usual plate of meat patties. I told the waiter to hurry and not forget the ketchup because we had a train to catch.

Soon, we took another leap onto the train as it inched out of the terminus and headed back to Dadar. I licked the remnants of the samosa around my lips, wiped my face on my sleeve, rubbed my tummy, and belched loudly, thoroughly satisfied. As the train jolted on the tracks and hurtled back home, my thoughts returned to the events of the day, starring Ma, Mrs. Karmarkar, and Prema. Suddenly, the train brakes screeched, and the momentum carried it forward for at least a mile. I was startled but relieved I was still on Dad's tummy. He put down the book and looked intently at me again as his eyes went sad and sentimental.

I told Dad I had one of the best rides of my life and begged him for an encore. He looked me in the eye with a wan smile and a deep hurt, which did not miss their intended target. I asked him what the matter was, and he answered after a lull.

"I nearly died, son, when Ma called and told me to hurry home."

I made the connection and looked away, welling. Ma must have gone to Kamath's restaurant and phoned Dad. I was deeply ashamed that today's misadventure had brought so much turmoil and unnecessary angst to my parents and me. Without further ado, he reminded me more convincingly than Ma did—he would not lose me to Sharad or anyone else.

I burst into tears as Ma, Elisabeth, and Narayan watched me as if death had invaded our home. I disappeared quickly, my face purple with shame, and hid under the little desk in our makeshift living room, watched over by Napoleon. I sat there whimpering in my train wreck. My heart stung with the effects of my self-sought banishment. I was thunderstruck again as I realized that Dad and Ma would never ever lose me to the likes of the Karmarkars. His words hurt me, hurt me worse than any rolled-up newspaper.

Years later, I heard that Sharad, bright as he was, never finished school and became one of Sawant's underlings. He never stood a chance in his broken home, and I was fortunate that I had my parents, who cared.

Chapter 8: Accident

Dad's accident occurred on Sunday, March 31, 1957, around 9 am on his way to an office picnic at Versova Beach, a remote fishing village in northwest Bombay. Together with March 30, the previous day, those two days remain forever intertwined. Like the Phantom's mask, the seamless transmogrification from happiness to utter hopelessness was so fleeting that only an optimist like Dad could have tackled it. A careless god tried to obfuscate us, or so it seemed at first. Beneath the mask was Dad's face, his eyes sparkling for battle.

Dad was a lifetime member of the JN Petit Library near his office, and so was John after he turned 12. The over-century-old Petit Library, built in 1856, features lancet-style black stone arches, intricate towers on the exterior, and splendid interiors with colored-glass windows, making it an impressive three-story Neo-Gothic stone structure. Saturdays being a half-day at work, Dad came home after a leisurely visit to the library. In its well-lit reading room, which demanded silence, Dad sprawled in the luxury of one of the easy chairs and read. He kept up with worldwide news and politics, making notes in his green notebook. He usually reached home after I returned from school, which finished at 4 pm, an hour early on Saturdays.

March 30, 1957, was unlike any other Saturday. When I reached home, Ma was humming in the kitchen, preparing tea, and Elisabeth was reading. I was surprised to see Dad snoring with an open book resting on the orb in the front room. I crept up close and woke him up.

After dusk, the four of us departed for Dadar TT. John rarely came out with us; he was not around anyway. First, we stopped at the Asiatic Agency, a store owned by Mr. Rao, which sold soap, toothpaste, and stationery items. We looked forward to seeing the kind old proprietor, who usually had a dust mop perched on his shoulder, ready to strike every imaginary speck of dust on his spic and span glass showcases. Mr. Rao and Dad knew each other well. They often discussed Bombay's plight, including its population size, the number of homeless children, and politics, before any transaction took place. Mr. Rao, with his short, white, porcupine-like hair, was quite old but held himself well. He had a stuttering problem and a slow, measured guttural intonation, and it took him a long time to say anything. His young, matriculated Malayali assistant talked to Ma while stealing glances at Elisabeth.

As we left the store with our purchases, Elisabeth complained to Ma about Mr. Rao's helper. Ma told her to ignore him. Ignore him? Who? How? I was not following the conversation. Like Mr. Rao, I asked in a slow and measured rasping monotone, in a Malayali accent, "Hey sister Elisabethé, what are you both talking about?"

Ma pealed with laughter at this while Dad guffawed, cheeks exploding.

Then she abruptly stopped and stared into the starlit sky, sure that a lightning bolt would strike her. All of this embarrassed Elisabeth, and she turned a deep shade of red.

The Jacobite Malayali store manager of the Bata Shoe Store next door waited to waylay Dad. As soon as we left Mr. Rao's store, he jumped off his stool and greeted us. If previous experience were any indicator, this would take a while. To our embarrassment, Elisabeth groaned succinctly. Luckily, we escaped from the store manager when his sales clerk came out to ask him a question.

Next, we visited our old grocer. We waited for our turn while a group of children played a prank on Dad. They pulled a thick jute rope through a hole in a can, causing it to sound like a growling dog. We all laughed at Dad's expense, and he joined in the fun. Dad could not stop laughing when he caught others reacting as he did. Every time they pulled this trick, it was hilarious to watch. Ma stopped and glanced heavenward again, her laughter cut short, replaced by worry. She wondered aloud if all this merriment was a harbinger of things to come.

"God, please don't make us cry tomorrow," she implored Him, looking up with quiet, dignified concern. She always pleaded with Him, and Dad teased her about it. He reminded her that he was too busy to listen, adding that none of them could reach him if they ever needed him, given the traffic from her. Ma replied in mock seriousness that losing her radio license would be better from overuse rather than misuse. After her oft-repeated repartee, she tilted up her nose in annoyance at being disturbed and supplicated some more. How she kept up the conversation with Him that Saturday worried me, and I wondered if she knew something was afoot. Brushing aside these thoughts, I walked a few steps ahead with my head tilted to the night sky and peered at the moon with my eyes scrunched to narrow slits.

"Elisabethé, look at the moon. It's following us," I said, still imitating Mr. Rao.

"Idiot," Elisabeth replied spontaneously, more out of habit than some newborn conviction based on evidence. Nevertheless, it still hurt, and I did not understand why she always had to behave like a snapping turtle with me. I looked back at Dad and Ma, my eyes glistening, and Dad proceeded to tickle me to wipe away the glisten.

I chuckled finally and said, "Do it again, Dad. Please."

Dad took hold of my hand, and we walked and talked together, father and son. He told me how far the moon was and informed me again that it revolved around the Earth.

"Does revolved mean going round and round something? Dad, you told me long ago that the Earth revolves around the Sun. Since the Moon revolves around Earth, it also means the Moon revolves around the Sun. Why, Dad, why? I am beginning to wonder why," I said, my words breathlessly racing, trying to catch up with my thoughts. I surprised Dad, taking hold of his hand and swinging our arms as high as they would go—back and forth—as if I did not have a care in the world.

We were both alone on a vast shore littered with beautiful seashells that lay ready for examination, one by one.

"You know, Dad, I think I know why."

I took a moment to reply when he asked me why. "Because the sky is too high," I giggled, buying time. "I know why. Every action has a reason; the Moon indirectly revolves around the Sun as it revolves around the Earth."

It was a simple case of cause and effect, albeit an indirect one. Dad gave my pithy discovery some thought. Finally, maybe realizing the point I was trying to make, he patted me encouragingly and let go of me to tell Ma my latest finding. He paused momentarily and held his hand out for Ma as she caught up with him. Nothing else mattered as long as Dad and Ma, the ones I cared for most, were proud of me. As if answering my thoughts, Elisabeth snorted like one of those curly-tailed piglets in a fairy tale, a delayed reaction to my hypothesis.

I looked back at Dad and Ma and decided that turning around and walking backward would be the best course of action. I could watch them and keep an eye on the moon. I had never seen Dad acting so affectionately with Ma in public as they walked together. Ma's lips fluttered as a few 'amens' escaped her lips. Dad said something to her before I turned around to walk normally. I could not see if she was about to cry or smile in the dim streetlight, but whatever Dad said changed her demeanor. She stopped short and held on to him.

I asked Dad a few years later whether Ma was sad or happy at what he told her that evening. It was dismay, he said, when he informed her Sequiera would give him a ride to the picnic the following morning and pick him up bright and early from Dadar TT. Dad likened it to riding in the lap of luxury.

Mr. Joseph Sequiera was a junior clerk in Dad's office and inherited a Ford Prefect. He was the only one in the office with a car. Even though Dad's Chit Fund had folded, Sequiera came home regularly to seek help with his problems or try to entice Dad with his latest get-rich scheme.

He parked the car in front of the liquor store and told me to be the lookout. That is all I needed: an invitation to look out the window. John was sure he used to come to show off the Ford Prefect and often engaged Sequiera about it. After Sequiera departed, John poked fun at him using automotive visuals, at which we all laughed heartily, especially Dad. John convinced me that Sequiera's shiny strands of curly black hair were steel springs dripping in engine oil. He likened his body to a pint-sized piston rod attached to an engine-sized head. My brother said that the lifeless pair of round, bulging gray eyes on Sequiera's pale, bloodless face was a hastily slapped-on afterthought, an apt description, I thought. He alluded to Sequiera being a devil and said the only missing parts were a pair of horns.

Early Sunday morning, I woke up to Dad droning 'From Greenland's Icy Mountains' as he readied himself. Soon, my ears perked up to their whispering.

"See, you've woken him. You better take him to the picnic, too."

"*Koché*, how can I? I am the only one Sequiera invited to enjoy the ride with his family."

"Why not take Mathew too, now that you have woken him up on Greenland's icy mountains? He will be so happy being with you and sad all day to find you gone."

Dad hurriedly hugged me, promising a big surprise if I was good, and added that the car was too full to take me. I pleaded and said that I would sit in his lap, which he said was unsafe. I left it at that since I had not even brushed my teeth.

Ma stood next to me by the window, our shoulders touching. In the rising sun's red glow, I saw she needed more consolation than I did. Dad finally looked back and waved before rounding the corner. Waving back sullenly, half-heartedly, and leaning into Ma, who gave me a reassuring squeeze, I remembered our happy family outing the day before, tempered with her cautions.

A few hours later, we heard a heavy-handed knock on our back door, and the unlocked door banged open as the door latch slammed against the wall. The person who barged in had never visited us before but lived on the floor below, around the stairs, right below Chinka's tenement. He was the diminutive and jocular Mr. Kanan, a Malayali Hindu, a watch-repairer at a watch store in Flora Fountain. He was shorter than Ma. When he was home, he would usually leave his front door wide open. He sat hunched over his round table, with his watchmaker's loupe in one eye and the other eye narrowed to a slit, examining watches. We passed his front door coming up or going down, and Dad and Ma sometimes stopped by and talked to the Kanans. Mr. Kanan always joked. During an idle banter, he had famously told Ma that repairing watches was not as simple as making rice and curry. Like most Indian men, the fellow had no idea what it took to make one of Ma's curries. He hurried to our bedroom and seemed impatient to tell us whatever he had on his mind.

The words would not come out, which I thought was unusual for him, as he was never at a loss for words. Behind him were two strangers attired in white, a man and a woman. Eerily enough, all three were in white. Elf-like, Mr. Kanan stood before the strangers, with his white vest and white lungi, inadequate in expressly announcing the visitors' names, and was tongue-tied for once. He was in shock, unsure what to say, as he searched for words and finally gave up. He determinedly pressed his trembling lips to a thin, dark streak and waited. I was facing the door as Ma turned around and saw all three, and her lips and face turned pale, drained of blood. Then the stranger said something to Ma, and he held her outstretched hands and eased her fall. Ma fell back and fainted. John and Elisabeth rushed from the front room. The stranger told Ma that Dad was in a severe accident, had lost his left arm, and was in Nanavati Hospital undergoing surgery. He had lost an enormous amount of blood. They left him after they took him to surgery. The whole scene—the visitors' appearance, Ma's reaction, and my siblings rushing—took seconds to play out and remains etched in my mind, embedded forever.

Before Ma and John rushed to the hospital, Ma gave Elisabeth many instructions. She also told me to heed Elisabeth and not leave the tenement for any reason. For once, I did not press Ma to take me with her, and before they hurried to the hospital, I kissed them both. Ma smiled at me through her tears. Everything stumbled so suddenly into place that lunch was the last thing on her mind as they hurried to the hospital. The morning, followed by the afternoon, wore on, and both of us got hungrier and hungrier.

Meanwhile, the strangers in white must have gone to our church, interrupted the service, and told the pastor about Dad. Somehow, word got around to the nearby Jacobite church as well. In her instructions, Ma had not taken into account the number of people coming to see us. Expecting to see Ma at home, many churchgoers were soon at our door. Elisabeth and I could not keep up with answering every knock on the door as the people from both churches trooped in. Finally, we left both doors to our tenement ajar to let them troop by.

Ma and John dropped by Uncle George's flat in Bandra on the way to the hospital to inform him what had happened to Dad. He was not home, so they left a message with his neighbor. Uncle George arrived soon after Ma and John reached the hospital. While the three waited outside the operating room, Uncle George and John talked to the hospital staff. He told them he would cover all expenses and even gave Ma some money.

For Dad, it was touch-and-go for the next 48 hours as they transferred him to critical care after his amputation, and his miraculous recovery got underway from the moment he opened his eyes. I held it together at school the day after, not telling the class teacher or classmates about Dad. After quenching my thirst at the water tank during recess, I stayed in my classroom, doing nothing, as the movie rolled out, frame by frame, showing the events from Saturday and Sunday. Daydreaming got the better of me as I thought of Dad and wondered what he looked like in his hospital bed without his arm and how I would tell him about everything he had missed while he was gone. I remembered our last walk together when I swung his left arm as far as it would go, which I would never be able to do again.

I also thought of Ma fainting and hitting the bed, how it scared me, and how quickly she got up and took charge. I knew Ma was extra special, and even though it seemed far-fetched, I believed she knew on Saturday that something was about to befall us soon.

Years later, a disquieting thought struck me: you must watch and listen to mothers like these. Lucky me, you say, to have mothers who can look you in the eye and offer their blistering insights, withering you with their love and thoughtfulness. Why are they so relentlessly spot-on and why do we ignore them to our detriment? Yes, why was their intuition so razor-sharp? That was my question, too, for which I never could find an answer.

Before the 48 hours were up, Dad's comeback was in full swing as he started eating, and he asked Ma to bring the children the next day. We went to the hospital on the third day. On our trip by bus, I relived Dad waving at us as he turned the corner that Sunday morning, and I felt awful that I hadn't waved back with my usual enthusiasm. The hospital was far away, so we got off at the bus stop in front of it and crossed the road. It was a white two-story concrete building with an entrance at the center of a roundabout and a well-tended flower garden. The hospital was not as busy or as big as the multi-storied government hospitals in the city.

Dad sat propped up in bed, surrounded by visitors. Matron Mary and Uncle George were among them. Dad's eyes lit up when he saw us as I ran to him and buried my head in his embrace, and he, in turn, held on to me, not wanting to let me go, while he kissed Elisabeth. I had never been happier, and the misgivings about what Dad might look like disappeared upon seeing him. Looking at my Dad, it was hard to tell that he had been through so much these few days, and here he was, in the center, recounting how it all unfolded. Ma had told me most of it, but coming from Dad, I knew I would never forget his story. Suddenly, the hopelessness gnawing in the pit of my stomach vanished, and I was happy to be alive, euphoric to hear his voice.

Dad described the events of that day with a detachment as if describing someone else's experience. Dad said he felt a sharp pain in his left side. Dad looked out the car window and realized the car had left the road and was stuck next to a lamppost. He looked at Sequiera, a man in a state of shock. His children were crying, and Mrs. Sequiera was screaming. Dad reached out to open the car door to get out, but could not move his left hand. That is when he realized his left arm was gone, and when he felt for it with his right hand, there was nothing but wetness—wet with blood.

Suddenly, a wave of calmness overcame his panic. It enveloped his whole being as he deliberately reached for the handle, opened the door, and got out. Looking around, he saw the car had skidded down from the road and landed past the lamppost into a shallow ditch. He climbed the slope, stepped onto the remote, traffic-less road, stood in the middle, and searched up and down, looking for help. Far away, he saw the first sign of hope—a red and white dot approaching him. It was a BEST public transport bus. Steadily, with blood streaming from his left side, he stood there waving for the bus to stop. The bus repeatedly honked as it approached, and the honking grew louder, but Dad refused to budge, and it came to a screeching halt. He climbed the bus and told the panic-stricken driver to hurry and take him to Nanavati Hospital. He turned around and told the passengers to get off. All of them did, except two, a man and a woman dressed in white.

The woman screamed that she recognized Dad from church and burst into tears; her husband remembered Dad, too. The bus driver said he had to take Dad to the police station, but Dad would not hear of it. The driver consented and drove maniacally to the hospital, six or seven kilometers away. Dad ran into the hospital emergency room and wailed for help. The doctors, the nurses, and the ward boys were all hands on deck as they hurried to assist. Dad was still fully awake when the orthopedist informed him that he would have to amputate the rest of his arm, to which Dad replied that he would do no such thing and that he had better leave a stump. He also instructed the surgeon to ensure the transfused blood was compatible. I learned about blood transfusion and its thorny issues just by listening to Dad talk about it on later occasions. As he went under, he gave the two in white our address to notify Ma. I had many questions, one in particular, but decided to mull them over.

As I listened to Dad, I realized there was so much more to this awe-inspiring man that I was beginning to fathom. There was no doubt in my mind that he would inspire me for the rest of my life and leave a lasting impact on the many people he had helped. I had no idea I would take on the challenge of narrating his story, not only the accident but also the inadvertent life lessons he had left me with and the hardships Ma and he had endured. I had no clue I would tell Dad's story the only way I could, one day, through a child's unfiltered eyes. I had humbly dared to put my feet in his shoes and tell people my story, excuse me, his story. Knowing my inner self through my Dad's struggles could only come through a creative process, such as writing about it. Maybe someday, it would be worthwhile if it saved another dumbass like me.

As Dad finished his narration, my mind drifted off. I did not hear the rest as the audience sprinkled Dad with questions. I also had to tell him so much, and I did not want to let go of this chance for his undivided attention. Once the commotion died down, I cleared my throat to get Dad's attention. With my elocution voice, nurtured by Dad and teachers alike who had successfully trained and won me school competitions, I began my story in a room of mostly strangers. I told Dad what he had missed since Sunday. Everyone listened in pin-drop silence.

I told him about Ma fainting and falling on the big bed when people dressed as angels visited us. I told him how Ma and John quickly dressed to leave, how I acted grown-up and didn't pester Ma to take me with her, and how I gave both a quick kiss instead. I noticed John wiping off my dry kiss. I described people from both churches who came before services finished and many more after church —they came home and clucked-clucked their way like chickens, looking for Ma. Not finding her, they made it worse for us with their long, sad faces, staring like we were museum exhibits, whispering to each other, and with hardly any words for us. As the afternoon wore on, the crowd grew, becoming more tiresome. Elisabeth decided to leave both doors unlatched, and I went to sleep hungry. Lily, an RN who had lived with us, visited us. Rendered speechless by the news, she guessed we had missed lunch and hastened to make rice and vegetables. I slept again after eating.

When I woke up late in the evening, John was home. I asked him about Ma and Dad. He told me Ma would come home late at night with Uncle George. He also told us that Dad was still asleep after the operation. Soon, John and Elisabeth were searching for something, and they told me there was a stink in the house. I said I could not smell a thing. They burst into laughter when they announced they had discovered feces neatly wrapped in a newspaper. I then explained that I was afraid to go to the bogs without Ma nearby. How Ma had told me not to leave the house, and how I minded that. I then took several Times of India sheets, conducted my business on them, and hid the package under the bed, intending to dispose of it outside in the trash. I forgot all about it, but did not forget to clean myself with soap and water, as Ma had taught me. I was sad at school the next day, but did not tell anyone, not even my class teacher. I promised to sleep beside Dad daily, lie down where his left hand used to be, and care for him forever. Everyone chuckled and sighed in relief when I finished my breathless outburst. Dad could not have been prouder of me as he smiled back weakly and squeezed my hand with all the strength he could muster. His tired eyes shut as he drifted to sleep with a smile.

⸺ ◉ ⸺

A RIPTIDE OF MEMORIES yanked me to the day we brought Dad back from the hospital. A hero's welcome was what awaited my Dad. I insisted on accompanying John this time to bring him home from the hospital. I told enquiring neighbors we were off to the hospital to bring Dad home. It seemed many already knew. As I waved at Ma and Elisabeth, I wondered whether that sullen boy who waved back disappointedly at his Dad as he trotted off to the picnic could ever wave again without thinking about that day. I suppose the word spread fast that Dad was coming home. Everyone in the building had heard of the accident, about Dad's bravery, and his presence of mind in commandeering the BEST bus to the hospital. Many had followed Dad's day-to-day progress. Some neighbors had even visited him in the remote hospital.

As we approached Sabita, I saw Ma and Elisabeth on the lookout for us. I noticed that the verandas on each floor had more residents than usual, all keeping a close eye out. To my surprise, they were all eagerly awaiting Dad. There was a large group at the entrance, and one of them opened the taxi door. I was at the head of the procession as we exited the taxi. John and Uncle George were behind me, guiding Dad, followed by the taxi driver, who carried Dad's belongings. In the crowd were Otta Kaiyan and Sawant's minions, cheering my Dad. For once, they were not at each other's throats. Our Parsi rent collector, Mr. Pestonji, was also standing by, sadly shaking his head as he saw Dad in his condition. Standing at the head of the stairs in the lobby was the imperious Sawant sahib, his palms held together in a respectful namaskar, and he spontaneously said a namasté. Dad smiled back weakly at them. The people responded to Sawant sahib's cue amid loud clapping and namastés. The crowds watching from the front balconies now spilled onto the railing on each landing, looking down as Dad climbed one painful stair after another. The story was the same on each floor. The fourth floor, above us, had emptied onto our floor. All my accomplices were there—Chinka, Sharad, Vijaya, and sweet Kamala. Even Sharad, who was forever my friend, even though, I could no longer play with him.

Neighbors wept. He had single-handedly brought everyone together: Hindus, Muslims, Christians, and Parsees alike. None of them had ever heard or seen anything like this. They were in awe of his miracle. I would miss them all if we were ever to leave Sabita. The mulling question I had about the accident would wait until he was well enough to talk. I did not realize that this black swan event was my first deeply ingrained mental stamp. In the ancient Pāli language during Gautama Siddhartha's time, such a mental imprint was similar to what they called a *saṅkhāra*, something that needs to be let go of or forgotten, such as a grievous hurt caused by oneself or inflicted upon oneself by another person. The difference was that mine was a mental stamp I would forever take inspiration from, rather than one that had to be let go of.

We used the kitchen entrance to the tenement to get into number 24. Deshmukh, he of the langots, and his family stood at their doorway with a welcoming smile. His clotheslines were bare, with no loincloths anywhere. Ma and Elisabeth were both at the door, weeping.

Dad recuperated quickly under Ma's excellent care. He regained his paunch and repertoire of jokes and returned to the unwelcome business of bathroom singing. Having left me that morning on Greenland's Icy Mountains, I did not hear that missionary song from him, and I sometimes sang it, not realizing I was reminding him that it was all right to sing it. What bothered him most was the ghost or phantom pains on his left side. He kept telling us it was getting worse, not any better.

He had a daily stream of visitors, well knowns and unknowns, and one particular admirer from the underworld–Sawant sahib. He visited him regularly until the day Dad returned to work. For each visitor, Ma made hot chai the way only Ma could. His high school classmate, Maliackel George Chandy, the then Veliatherumeni or head of the Mar Thoma Church, came to see him with much fanfare. Ma made some fantastic snacks with coffee for the honored one, and she let me sample them as the only member of the tasting committee.

My career goals changed based on the spread Ma prepared for the VIPs. First, I wanted to be a church vicar, the first step to becoming a bishop. After Madhavan's visit, who was in line to become Bombay's Mayor, I heard the call to join the Municipality of Bombay. I wanted to one day be the Kerala Chief Minister (CM) after EMS, the soon-to-be CM of Kerala, visited Dad. Finally, I gave up because it was hard keeping up with the constantly changing career paths that beckoned me. Keeping our visitors fed and hydrated cost a fortune because, finally, when the stream trickled down to zero, it was back to our prior lifestyle. Ultimately, I knew that tinkering with stuff was what I liked to do most.

AS I LISTENED TO DAD'S recounts of the accident, I recalled a nugget from the morning of the panic, sorry picnic. When Dad hurried to Mr. Joseph Sequiera that morning, Joseph seemed fidgety as he stood there with a cigarette dangling from his lips and one foot proprietarily propped up on the car fender. He turned to look at his watch when he spotted Dad and returned Dad's friendly waves with a fierce scowl. Dad felt his friend offered a ride more out of duty, as one of his subordinates, rather than out of genuine friendship. Dad felt insulted, swore he would never make the same mistake again, and regretted not acting instinctively. He should have told Sequiera that he had changed his mind, turned around, walked home to get me, and used public transport to take us to the picnic. When he finished, he patted his left-hand stump, a memory that is still vivid for me. Why, Dad, I wanted to ask, why did you not follow your instincts? That Sunday and the rest of our lives would have been so different had you listened to your inner voice! Was getting a ride in that heap so important, or did you not have the heart to brush off the overbearing Mr. Joseph Sequiera and return home for us?

AS A TEENAGER, AFTER thumbing through the pages of Dad's green cloth-bound notebook, I asked him whether he planned to write about the accident. He said it would all happen in good time. He told me something he had withheld from me all this time, his thoughts after he waved to us that fateful morning. He said it was something I was too young to comprehend, especially its evil side. Dad told me this: He felt sad when he turned to wave and saw Ma consoling me. He thought of how Ma and I had fended off one of our Malayali neighbors, who tried to molest her. I was napping one afternoon when the fellow came to have tea with Ma. He followed Ma into the kitchen and grabbed her by the pallu of her sari. She turned around, alarmed, and backed into the kitchen, grabbing a *kathi* (knife). Brandishing the knife, Ma repeatedly screamed that she would hurt him if he came any closer.

Dad told me I woke up at Ma's screams and rushed to the kitchen, and I scared the assailant, who ran right past us and out of our tenement through the crowd of angry neighbors behind the door who had heard Ma's screams. I had a hazy recollection of the talk relating to the event—about a knife, Ma, and the lout—but I did not know I was present. Maybe it was my way of coping, backed up in my mind, recalled but vaguely. The lout habitually visited us in the evenings, well talced and shaven after a bath. He talked to Ma and me while my siblings ignored him.

As Dad walked to meet Mr. Sequiera, he shuddered at the thought of the incident. At the same time, his chest filled with pride for both of us. He thought of how the two of us had thwarted the devil incarnate. He wished he had taken both Ma and me to the picnic.

I harbored deep resentment toward the neighbor; his name and face would forever be stuck in my subconscious. In 2009, I visited Sabita Building with my college classmate. The security person at the building entrance produced a ledger, opened it to the page listing the residents, extended it to me, and asked whom I was visiting. I quickly scanned the names and came across the only one familiar on the list—that of the lout. Without missing a beat, I lied. We were there to see him. I was shocked that he was still alive and had never left that hovel.

We knocked on the door of his tenement. The door opened. Before us stood a hard-to-recognize, half-naked, lungi-clad, hirsute, wiry, dark-skinned old man with a protruding rib cage. Then, the talcum smell hit me, and I knew it was he. His wife was there, too, although she seemed not to be all there. I told him who I was, and he remembered me from 52 years ago. We talked back and forth about his son, now a big shot who lived next door. It looked like the apple could not escape the tree. During the conversation, I felt sick and awash with mixed emotions: fear, disgust, and anger. I did not understand how this shriveled-up man could still invoke fear. Blood rushed to my head, my face became hot and sweaty, and my hair stood on end. I intertwined my fingers because I did not trust what my mind was telling me to do—strangle him NOW, it said. I nearly lost it that day. I made a hasty retreat, dragging my friend along without any explanation. I was glad I had taken my friend with me. We rushed out to the Muslim restaurant and had a cold drink to cool down, followed by lunch.

⸻ ◉ ⸻

DAD WAS HOME THE SECOND week of April, and well-wishers petered out by the following week. On Easter Sunday, April 21, 1957, Ma attended church service and came home with the angels. I call them angels because not only have I forgotten their names, but they were also Dad's guardians, and by extension, ours. The angels watched Dad in open-mouthed astonishment, as he appeared so cheerful and healthy.

I shudder at what might have happened had Dad taken me on that car ride from hell. Then I thought of something uplifting—like the evening we brought Dad home—how Easter's promise was ahead of schedule. I am sure Dad realized the significance of the angels' visit on Easter Sunday. He single-handedly refused his appointment with the dervish from Samarra so Ma and he could continue their mission with us in tow.

The angels did not stay long and came to invite us to their flat in Versova the following Sunday. After they left, we had our Easter Sunday meal, consisting of rice, yogurt curry, potato chips, and Ma's incomparable dry, fried boiled-duck-egg curry, made with ingredients typically used in meat dishes. Although it was a simple meal, as Easter feasts go, it was most memorable because we had Dad for the celebration. Dad had kept his promise when he brought himself to us after the picnic—the biggest and best surprise of all, especially for me.

During his fast recovery, Dad spent some of his waking moments in deep thought to the point we were all getting concerned. Ma prayed quite a bit and had no time to smile. The more he talked about the accident to visitors, the more time he spent brooding. He was depressed and frustrated, bemoaning why this hiccup in our lives happened. He said he could not get the circumstances of the accident out of his head, no matter what. He could not understand the freak accident, the whys, and the wherefores. He knew he was very sleepy when he felt a sharp pain on his left side as the car went off the road and came to a stop by the lamppost. Why did the lamppost cleave his arm? That was Dad—always thinking. We were left baffled by all his whys.

Dad was excited about the forthcoming Sunday outing to visit the angels. He would show us the accident site and then visit our angels. His enthusiasm had me chomping at the bit, too. I had questions that required a logical explanation. It would test my recent postulation—the 'every action has a reason' bit. Of course, the accident served no useful purpose but to waylay a family. Still, there was a reason why it happened. Maybe our trip would reveal some of the answers. As the bus started on Versova Beach Road, Dad looked out the window anxiously. Finally, there was a point when he yelled to the driver to stop so we could get off. The bus stopped, and we got off.

As the bus receded into the sunset and became a silhouette, before me, as far as the eye could see, stretched a lonely country road with equally spaced lampposts on the side. I held Dad's arm with all my strength as he unsteadily stepped off the gravel, and the two of us walked up and down a few times, looking for the lamppost. Ma and Elizabeth stood by watching.

"This is the one," he finally whispered as he examined the stains on the post. Dad, like a tour guide, explained what happened. We walked around the lamppost a few times, as Dad looked around in deep thought. Soon, he came to some conclusions, decided it was time to leave, and left us in suspense. Ma stood there, hands held together in silent prayer, tears streaming down her cheeks. Dad stood there in total silence, unflinching–suppressing, I suppose, his urge to tease Ma. As I strained my eyes, mesmerized by the top of the cenotaph-like lamppost that spawned my father's heroic acts, I felt his grip tighten, which brought me back to terra firma. Dad was still next to me, tugging, ready for us all to go back to the bus stop. I closed my eyes as we walked together, hand in hand, and imagined and relived the accident again.

Soon, we arrived at the angels' flat, and after tea and snacks, we sat around and talked for a little bit. They seemed like they had not been married too long since they had no children. To them, I was a curiosity. I sat between the angels, answering their questions, and I could see they liked me. Dad and the angels talked about the seminal event of our lives while I went around the living room looking for something to play with or read. During the lull in the conversation, I asked the one question I had wanted to ask Dad at the hospital during my first visit.

"Dad, I can't understand one thing," I said. "I wanted to ask this question for a long time."

I went and sat between the angels, holding their hands tightly. They were my angels, too. Dad asked me if he had missed or forgotten something, he should have mentioned.

"You didn't miss anything. No, you did. You missed something," I said, looking up at the angels with my eyes darting from one to the other, still holding their hands.

"Why didn't Uncle tear Auntie's sari and bandage your arm so the blood would stop?"

Looking at their surprised faces, I saw my question had stumped them.

"That is a question for the ages. Out of the mouths of babies," Dad exclaimed as his voice trailed off. Both angels cuddled me. I got goosebumps as the missus spontaneously kissed me on both cheeks like Ma. The fact is, they had not thought of applying a tourniquet.

After a nice dinner and togetherness, we knew it was time to depart. The angels accompanied us on our ride to Andheri Railway Station. Sitting beside Dad on the bus, he called me a deep thinker and took pride in me. He said that, for once, someone smart had commented on his story. He said that what usually got his goat from the visitors to his bedside was wringing hands, followed by contorted faces looking heavenward with praises to the Lord and irrelevant questions. He was sure all their reactions and responses were well intended. He told me I was the only one who had asked the only question that mattered. I felt a welling in my chest at the shot of confidence he bestowed on me! As the bus hurtled past the accident site, the missus nudged Ma, and they both made a sign of the cross. They helped Dad get on the train and ensured we were all comfortable before they departed. I am sad to say we lost touch with them after moving from Dadar. They, indeed, were one of a kind. Visits to the church became less frequent as taking care of Dad became the primary mission.

After we visited the accident scene, Dad's mood and disposition improved. In his mind, he had answers to most of the questions he had posited earlier during his days of healing. I soon knew why Dad had become almost his usual self when he told us about the mind-boggling discovery he had made at the accident site. The lamppost that severed his hand was a salvaged rail. Dad had seen many rail lines in the railway yards when he investigated goods shipment issues as a claims clerk for the BPT Railways. He knew them like the back of his hand. Indeed, the whole row of lampposts on the road to the beach was rail lines, and each stood on the road with its flat, tapering flange facing traffic, each a deadly guillotine waiting for a new victim. Indeed, it was a negligent substitution when the British Raj paved the remote road and installed lampposts, each mindlessly substituted to save the cost of re-smelting the spent rail. Dad was sure the British would not have gotten away with such carelessness in their country. I think I knew what he would do next—fight the system.

⟹◉⟸

JOHN'S JUNIOR BSC EXAMS, held a few weeks after Dad's accident, went well. Medical colleges interviewed him two months later, and he accepted admission to the Christian Medical College (CMC) in Punjab. A couple of months later, he was off to college.

The day before he left for college, Matron Mary came to see him and wished him success. She even gave him thirty rupees for his books. I remember Mary's beaming face well when she told John how proud she was of him and how wonderful it was to know he would soon be the first doctor from the Marthomite community.

She expressed the hope that Elisabeth would become our first female doctor. As for her godson, she said, the rumor was that he was quite the tinkerer. Dad and Ma could not have been prouder of us.

Dad could not do anything he used to do without our help. His helplessness frustrated him. Ma worked hard to keep him happy, reining in his impatience as best as possible. Joyfully, Ma and Elisabeth helped him with his everyday chores, never considering them a burden. I put in my bit, too. I helped him with his socks and shoes almost daily and tickled his soles often to make him smile. On occasion, I polished his shoes, as well as mine. Sadly, though, Dad could not easily handle the encumbrances of living in a third-floor tenement with its stairs, narrow confines, and shared toilets. He was too far gone after his accident to live in the tenement. Several months after Dad's accident, we moved to the BPT Officers' Railway Quarters in the remote suburb of Wadala, near Bombay, several miles from Dadar, where I lived until I was 17. Nostalgia for Dadar followed me to Wadala. I would miss Chinka, Vijaya, Kamala, and even Sharad. I would miss all my fun-filled celebrations with the Sabita community, such as Diwali, Janmashtami, Holi, and Dussehra, when exchanging friendship leaves of the Apta tree among children took place, as well as Bakr-Id, Ramadan, Easter, and Christmas. Moving was bittersweet. Not even a bungalow could easily replace the dreadful tenement.

———◆———

DURING ALL THIS TIME, the constant drumbeat of events in my life continued unabated, and it yanked me along for the ride. After Dad's untimely passing eight years later, I recalled many of those events, tinged with great life lessons even though, to others, they may appear trivial.

———◆———

CHAPTER 8 PICTURES:
1. Dad's green notebook
2. Pages from the notebook

Dad made notes from the books he read. Although his cursive is hard to decipher, what is noteworthy, if you look closely, is that he was reading books by Bertrand Russell and others. Dad did not limit his reach to philosophers and politicians. On the adjacent page, he mentions Ivan Turgenev, a Russian novelist and short story writer. I was awestruck and saddened. He had so much more to tell me.

In 2023, I met my 91-year-old, healthy first cousin, who had lived with us as a 17-year-old for several months while job seeking. Dad published at least one book. He told me he toted loads of hardcover books to a downtown bookstore. These books had Dad's name, E. K. Daniel, imprinted on them.

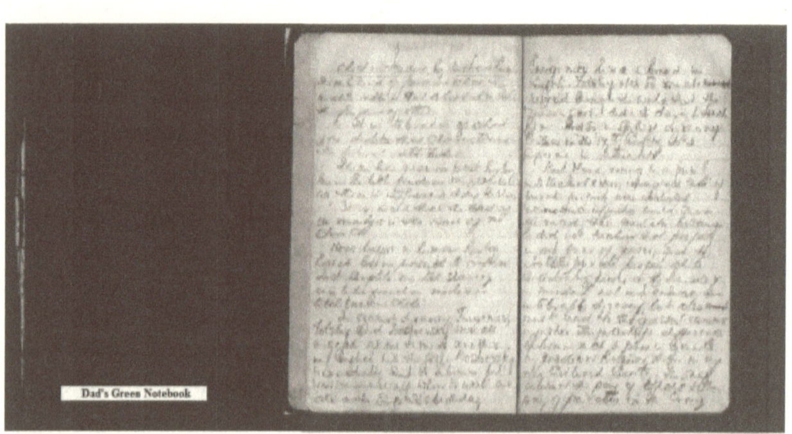

Chapter 9: Tenement to Bungalow

We moved to the BPT officers' bungalows in Wadala, a suburb of Bombay, some miles from Dadar. It was self-contained, with running water, three large rooms, an open front veranda facing Reynolds Road, a large kitchen next to the back veranda, which overlooked a kitchen garden, and its servants' quarters. What made it beyond belief was that Reynolds Road had a free dispensary and a clubhouse with amenities including table tennis, billiards, badminton, and outdoor basketball. We took it all in strid —even the bloodthirsty mosquitoes, the 24/7 BPT goods railway yard operations' all-pervading noise, soot pollution, and the daily 40-minute walk to and from Wadala station, which left us tired, albeit healthier. We thought nothing of all these inconveniences since it was all about Dad's well-being that had come at a high price—his arm.

Reynolds Road ran north-south on a strip approximately one and three-fourths miles long and about 300 feet wide, from the station to the No. 6 railway crossing. A metal picket fence and the BPT Railway quarters flanked it. Beyond the fence were the Harbour commuter lines and the BPT railway lines. Behind the quarters were the shunting yards operating day and night. We lived in bungalow B1 (2) a mile south of the railway station; a turnstile in the fence in front of our home allowed access past the railway lines and slums to Kidwai Road.

Dad righted wrongs whenever and wherever. After our move, Dad studied the B-type bungalows and informed our upstairs neighbor that he had no right to half our garden. Mr. Karnik vacated it without much argument, remained friends, and we ended up with the same-sized garden as the other ground-floor neighbors in the B-type quarters.

Next on Dad's list was the open front veranda. It had no protective grill; we sweltered in the heat and humidity most nights since we had to shut the front doors facing the road. The authorities acted upon Dad's complaints and installed a protective grill around the front ground-floor verandas on all B-type quarters, which resolved the problem, provided additional security, and increased our living space by a third.

Then came the big one—Dad's civil claim for the accident, for which I had a ringside seat. The lawyer he hired kept harping, 'There is no case, Mr. Daniel.' Not easily deterred, Dad was a persistent plaintiff. The lawyer came around with a growing respect for his remarkably erudite client. Dad was in his element as he helped the lawyer, like an éminence grise, with the oral arguments. The fight lasted a few rounds and almost half a year before the judge came around. The bureaucracy took its time. A year and a half later, it awarded Dad fifteen thousand rupees, a well-deserved judgment. Besides awarding Dad, the ruling required the replacement of all the razor-edged lampposts. On a trip to Bombay in 2013, I went to Versova to check if they had replaced the lampposts. After over five decades, the fishing village was an unrecognizable urban jungle. Confused and lost, I left with one consoling thought—all the lampposts I saw during our hour-long search in the motorized rickshaw were round posts.

Dad paid off John's and Elisabeth's medical college fees in arrears, bought second-hand furniture, including a sofa set, our first radio, and an old Singer electric sewing machine for Ma, and, after much pestering, enrolled me in drawing classes. Although Dad ironically remarked that losing his hand was not so bad, he would not wish it on anyone.

The drawing lessons were my first fee-paying extracurricular school activity, and my artistic aspirations got a much-needed boost. I passed the elementary and intermediate statewide government-conducted drawing exams with flying colors. Tinkering with the mechanics of the sewing machine led me to sew, and I sewed three sofa covers when the old covers soon fell apart, saving Dad the expense. Dad and Ma could not have been prouder of their 11-year-old.

⎯⎯●⎯⎯

MY FEAR OF THE TOILET vanished because it was our own and had a functioning flush. The BPT street-sweeping and toilet-cleaning staff, all Dalits, came every other day to clean our toilet and bathroom with phenyl disinfectant. Ma served them tea after their task, which I doubt any of our neighbors did.

The cleaning staff struck work for higher wages, leaving us high and dry. As the strike continued, I stepped up and cleaned the toilet, surprising my parents. I cleaned as best I could with the small amount of phenyl the staff had left us. In Gandhi's autobiography, the first serious book I had read, 'you had to set the example, be the change agent, and there was dignity in all work.' That is what my parents had taught me, too. The strikers caved when they learned that they could soon lose their jobs. With their wages garnished for the missed work, they were worse off than before. How sad and unfair the world was for the poor and defenseless.

The officers' servants lived in the E-type Servants' Quarters. My parents employed a widowed Maratha woman to do the household chores and errands for a monthly wage and a tenement in the 'E' Quarters. She had two young daughters, Shanti and Kusum, and a married son. The son's wife, Savitri, helped Ma during the mornings and afternoons and brought my school lunch. Shanti and Kusum dropped out of school in their teens, soon worked in houses, and took turns helping Ma. They became my good friends. During holidays, they worked quickly, and we played hide-and-seek and tag at home, fooling around in the backyard while tending to Ma's garden and hens. They were laying hens at that. I recently realized that Ma most likely took up poultry because of my weakness for eggs. That first summer, she showed off her poultry skills. The mother hen sat day and night on her eggs in our large, wide-mouthed bronze utensil in the corner of Dad's bedroom. According to Ma, day 21 was the big day. We hustled next to the angry hen with widening eyes as she gently tapped and cracked the eggs one by one. Cute chirping fluffs popped out as they pushed their way out, one by one, as Ma had predicted. The chicks stayed indoors for a few weeks, tweeting all day as we followed them, caring for and cleaning after them. Ma allowed them to roam with the mother hen in our garden a few weeks later. They came home at dusk to roost in Ma's two-story coop on our back veranda.

Ma created a lusher garden. To the backyard's white fragrant flowering tree, mango, banana, custard apple, *muringa*, and *mehndi* (henna) bush, she recreated Kerala, adding papaya, tapioca, chili, bitter gourd, beans, tea rose, and jasmine. Indeed, I learned most of my gardening and cooking skills from her. She nurtured everything she touched, including me.

The year we moved, Elisabeth passed high school with a first-class. Soon, Dad and Ma, with gritted

teeth, smiled at the community members who wanted to know when Elisabeth would be married off. My father's actions were as unique as the mannequin scene in Francisco de Goya's satirical El Pelele (1791-1792), which depicts four young women repeatedly bouncing a male straw figure representing chauvinism up and down in the air with a sheet of cloth until they dismember it. He chose a different path in a society where it was the norm to marry off girls. He sent my sister to Sophia College, Bombay's best women's college, after she finished high school in 1958. This decision, so rare for its time, led her to become the community's first female physician. In effect, he told his peers to welcome modernity.

My duties as Ma's helper changed overnight since Elisabeth was always too damn tired after her back and forth from the faraway college. I helped her too: ironed her clothes, did the dirty work of catching and killing cockroaches in soapy water for her to dissect, did her homework drawings of specimens, and made wax slabs for mounting the dead roaches and rats.

Although she was a bit too old for us, Elisabeth even played tag with Shanti, Kusum, and me. Shanti and I even manufactured 'cigarettes' from the herb *ajwain* (carom) wrapped in newspaper squares. We smoked them in the kitchen when Ma was not around, even as Elisabeth watched us, disgusted. Shanti came home and continued working even after she got married. Kusum married and moved far away. Elisabeth left home and went off to the same medical college as John.

My mischievous ways continued unabated. My unspent energies sought new subjects. Of all people, I was the chink in Dad's armor for a short time, as he became my victim. My father's helplessness did not stifle the child in me. That bully, that heartless, mischievous bounder, denied Dad what he needed. It culminated one evening when I unraveled the towel I wrapped around him. As he stood naked before me, I ladled the insult with a child's mocking laughter. I still cry when I read these lines, when I crossed a line. No one else was laughing, and Dad's eyes told me he was hurt beyond words. I retrieved the towel and wrapped him back quick, with a sigh. I stood there, head cowered down, devastated in sublime sorrow. I asked myself, what else was the little prick capable of? Sulking away, I lay face down and cried to sleep, ignoring Ma's and Dad's pleas to have dinner. There is nothing like a growling stomach to punish oneself—it came right out of Gandhi. Taking care of Dad became my primary mission.

Our confidence shattered—the accident cast a long shadow over our mornings. Quiet support and reflection replaced laughter and hurried goodbyes.

Dad tried to read the Times sitting on the sofa, but his handicap hindered him from doing so. He spread it on the veranda floor, sitting almost cross-legged, leaning on his palm to steady himself. I say 'almost' since he could not sit fully cross-legged without losing balance. I kept vigil from my desk by my wickets while reading the sports section or a storybook. Once he finished, he got off the floor as I stood by, ready to assist. Watching this daily event, I had an idea for a poem, and I had the first stanza scene of 'pot-bellied Papa sitting on the floor' back then, when I was nine, soon after Dad's accident. It started as a song with an original tune that I'd hum. That line of the poem, I realize, wasn't just a memory; it was the very spark that needed a book—needed stoking and nurturing—into the story you're reading now. I wrestled with the words, slow in their coming, welling up without stop, while thinking of the bright side of a memory from a long time ago. I went through several titles for the poem. Then, in a flash, a highly relevant title related to Dad's daily morning routine of scanning the headlines appeared. At the same time, Ma and I waited for him to finish, hoping a headline would not catch his eye and make him read the associated article.

Headlining Mornings with Dad and Ma

Pot-bellied Papa, tottering on the floor,
Bracing his arm to prevent a slip,
While phantom pain exacts a toll.
When in his early forties, he severed his arm,
Fate fractured our world forever in two.

Scanning the Times, the going slow,
Dad echoes headlines; a storm in a thimble, say I!
Growling, snapping, laughing, shaking at times,
At Nehru, trumpeting another grand plan.
"Why not let him strut?" I ask, not as bright as Dad.

Nearly twelve, I wait; hurry, Dad, hurry,
My eyes dart from the Sports section to Dad.
Soon, Ma calls; the water's hot; come get it, dear!
"Coming, Mama!" Dad, gently bathed, glows,
"Well done," he says. Always, Dad, I've got to run now,
Ahead awaits a long walk, a bus ride, before First Bell.

Memories alive, faded tapestry to wit,
Tempus fugit, our bond forever fit.

The ritual of Dad reading the newspaper remained, though his elocution voice sometimes tremored synchronized with his ghost pains.

Meanwhile, in the kitchen, Ma heated water for his bath. I helped with his clothes and towel. Ma yelled for me to get the hot water. While Dad waited, I ran to the kitchen and lifted the aluminum vessel off the stove. Holding the rim on both sides with a cloth, I walked gingerly to the bathroom, struggled to keep the utensil on an even keel, poured the water into the bucket, and mixed it with tap water. The hot water scalded Ma and me so often that we kept Neba-sulph handy to treat tiny but severe burns. After several nasty burns, we took the leaky bucket to the kitchen, poured the boiling water into it, and hurried it by the handle to the bathroom.

I helped with his bath and assisted him to the living room, where Ma had arranged his clothes, shoes, and socks. His hand fumbled with the shoehorn, frustration creasing his brow. I offered help, but he shook his head, determined to try again. He had breakfast and tea without assistance and left home for the railway station, a 15 to 20-minute walk away. One of us stood at the door, waving back and forth, as he disappeared around the bend on Reynolds Road. Dad usually returned late in the evening. Then, we repeated the morning bath routine. We often ate together. I was a slow eater, and so was Elisabeth. We usually had a good conversation during our meals. Dad would be the first to finish, and we proceeded to the bathroom to wash up as we lingered talking to Ma. As he passed by, he stopped to kiss Elisabeth and me on the back of our heads. He picked food from our plates with each peck, which I did not mind as long as he didn't peck and steal too many times. Then we sat around Ma as she read the Bible and Dad prayed. Elisabeth and I raced through the Lord's Prayer.

An incident soon after the towel inanity affected me for life. While coming home from school, my routine consisted of catching the BEST bus and getting off at Wadala Railway Station. I went into the station, walked the length of the platform, stopped by the tracks, crossed the railway lines when safe, reached the start of Reynolds Road, and walked home.

On my way home one evening during rush hour, when the trains were more frequent, I walked down the ramp of the northbound platform. I glanced down the rail lines and saw no approaching northbound train. I stood, mind adrift, with both feet planted on the northbound track, intently watching the southbound train crawling out of the platform. Suddenly, behind me, I heard blood-curdling screams. I jerked around to see the northbound train barreling toward me. I heard not the blaring train horns but the screaming people hanging from the train's doors less than fifty feet away. In sheer terror, I dived backward from the track and landed in the brush—a second tragedy averted by a whisker—by the luck of the draw. The train passed and screeched to a halt seconds later. Passengers, passersby, and the train guard soon surrounded me.

There was a collective sigh of relief when they found me unharmed. I dusted myself off, picked up my school bag, and walked off, sick of myself. I would not cry, not in front of strangers. I told Dad and Ma about it in the evening, and that is when we wept uncontrollably. Dad held me as he soothed me while Ma kissed me repeatedly. That night, I lay in bed with Dad. The following morning, we held each other, afraid to let go, and then he told me I should use the station footbridge to cross the commuter railway lines.

I hated using the bridge because a few lepers who had escaped from the nearby Acworth Leper Colony were usually among the beggars who sat under the covered bridge's shade. They often reached out to touch passersby with their oozing stumps. I was afraid of such an encounter, especially in my shorts. Several months later, Dad met me as I emerged from the bridge on my way home from school. He greeted me proudly, knowing I had heeded his words. The lepers remained my secret. I looked at their horrific faces as I passed by every day. Suffering was all around me, so why should I avoid it? Why should I shun it? Understand their pain, Mathew. The world is a lot uglier than you think.

I grew up in a hurry during this time. The two incidents, dropping the towel on Dad and my brush with death, happening as they did so close together, hit me hard. As for unsung heroes, like Dad, I would like to thank at least one person representing the blur of faces on the crowded train, who screamed an 11-year-old to safety. In the same breath, a thanks to the bold BEST bus driver, who changed his mind and drove like a mad man at the risk of severe reprimand or worse—and whose actions on March 31, 1957, saved someone I so dearly loved.

Every day was precious. I promised I would never mistreat Dad. To become Ma's able assistant at eleven became an unconditional contract. I never wandered off the trail again. I reminded myself of the privilege of being in the company of saints. I should have known better. I remained the court jester of the Daniel household, but my antics became more self-deprecating. I was still a little prick, but I was an endearing one. Even Ma noticed my change, and I felt lucky that Dad and Ma were still with me, allowing me to tap into their well of wisdom and spirituality, and perhaps, by mere osmosis, claim some of it for my own.

———◦———

AS I GREW OLDER AND taller, I became a better helper. My bond with my parents, as well as my self-esteem and self-discipline, strengthened. I teased and played with them as friends, even as I kept a wary eye on myself, never overdoing it as I did in the towel incident.

I learned about questioning authority from Dad, who had fought many battles. One, in particular, was the accident litigation he won. I heard he even wrote to Gandhi, questioning him, and Gandhi obliged him with replies he penned himself. Gandhi was long gone when I was growing up, and the Mahatma's legend awakened my curiosity about him from an early age. When I was old enough to use the library, Gandhi's autobiography, 'The Story of My Experiments with Truth,' was among the first books I read. I admired him and tried to emulate his legendary self-discipline.

Questioning elders proved helpful and aided me in choosing my skirmishes. I still remember the thrill I felt the first time I unwittingly put Dad's lessons into practice when confronted by a grievous injustice. It happened twice; the first time was after I entered sixth grade at ten and a half, and the second time a few months later, when the PT (physical training) teachers took away our free period because a few of my mates misbehaved in the queue. Punishing all 50 was simply unjust. During our free periods, we could play football, cricket, marbles, or loaf around on the playground instead of PT. Our PT teachers, Mr. Potnis and Mr. Kakirde, revoked the free period. I rushed off to Principal Drego and complained. Mr. Drego and I hurried to the PT hall. The teachers could not justify their disciplinary action, so Mr. Drego immediately overruled them. My classmates rushed out to the school grounds, whooping and hollering as I stayed back, and I let it all sink in before I ran out at the tail end. When it happened again, I hoped another kid would take up the cause, but no such luck, as my classmates egged me on and I obliged. The same scenario repeated itself with the same results. Seeing them happy again filled me with goosebumps. I realized that if it was a just cause, so was remedying it.

To his enormous credit, Mr. Kakirde never held a grudge. He was my eighth-grade Marathi teacher, and I became one of his favorites. He helped me and loved being my mentor because of my difficulty with the language, and he earned my respect as my teacher. He did not mind what I did in sixth grade and admired me for standing by my principles.

⸻ ◉ ⸻

THE ACCIDENT WAS A turning point in our lives. Although our move nearly killed me, it was ultimately beneficial that we made the move. Dad's well-being was what mattered.

Occasionally, I emulated Dad's one-handed life, performing my daily routines using only my right hand and immobilizing my left. I could not do it for long. Moreover, the ghost pains that nagged him were impossible to imagine. I could not simulate the sense of imbalance he constantly fought for the remainder of his life. I was awestruck by how my optimistic Dad carried himself for the next eight and a half years. He would remain a source of inspiration by his example as my plotline perilously veered off-course, and I had to get back on track in a hurry using the mansions he had built for me.

⸻ ◉ ⸻

CHAPTER 9 PICTURE.

    1. Seated: Grandma, center with Ma, Elisabeth on her right, and Aunt Sara, John on her left.

    2. Standing: Dad (behind Ma) and Uncle George

Chapter 10: Fame's Double-Edge

After Dad's accident, his star and fame ascended. After church services, people milled around my parents and greeted them. They latched on to Dad's every word. Even his detractors joined in the adulation. The fact that John was now in medical college added to the folklore. Elisabeth was soon to follow John. Then, Dad fought and won the civil lawsuit against all odds. I, too, basked in Dad's limelight. Some even talked to me. I think of it now as the Lazarus effect he had on our community. Church affairs ran more smoothly. His fame spread and permeated the other Malayali communities.

Meanwhile, Grandpa (Dad's father) and Grandma (Ma's mother) clamored to see him. They had visited us a few years earlier, and it was a fun-filled time. Grandma always sat with her hands on her lap, almost like steadying herself in a rocking boat as you can see in the picture at the end of the previous chapter. In her memory, I emulated her whenever I posed for pictures. I remember the haircut Grandpa had during his stay. He did not know a word of Hindi, and Narayan tricked him into saying '*sub kato*' when the barber asked him how he wanted his hair done. Grandpa came home without a hair on his head. 'Sub-kato' in Hindi meant 'cut all of it.' Dad celebrated the haircut, or should I say hairless cut, by having a studio picture taken of a clean-shaven Grandpa and me. Dad sent copies of the iconic photo to his Brethren relatives, and many to his nephew for distribution. The nephew missed the memo about what to do with those celebratory photographs and lopped me off without a thought, and many received a picture only of a shaven Grandpa. Years later, I probably stumbled on why they lopped me off.

Dad saved enough for a trip to Kerala to see my grandparents, three and a half years after the accident, when I was 12. We traveled in style, first-class coupe both ways. Dad received a substantial discount by proving that he was eligible for a railway discount as a railway employee, even though he wasn't a Central Railway employee, which catered to South India.

I recall meeting Grandpa, my old cousin, and Cruella, a wheezy, harried-looking, gray-haired woman. Grandpa would not let Dad out of his sight, and Dad enjoyed every minute of it. My elder cousin was the second kid from Dad's village to finish high school and speak English fluently. Dad tried getting him to come to Bombay and work, but he was immovable. Dad was stuck with helping him, thus enabling his Brethren lifestyle. He never left Kerala, except when he immigrated to join his children. I knew Cruella through Dad's improvised songs, but I did not make the connection when I first saw her. She struggled to breathe most of the time. Perhaps that was why everyone left her alone, including Dad, who barely spoke to her. The cousin had five or six school age children with whom I played, and we skinny-dipped under the waterfall at the edge of the forest across the road, becoming inseparable.

We then stayed with Grandma (Ma's mother) for several days. Grandma, her widowed daughter-in-law, and Ma's two older sisters, who came from far away, gave Dad and us a tremendous welcome. Each was a superb cook, and every meal they made in Dad's honor was a feast. I now knew where Ma learned to cook so well. We went back to Grandpa for the last few days. Before sunrise, we boarded the bus and headed to Chenganoor Railway Station for the train to Bombay via Madras. We knew we would be passing Grandma's home, and on the way, a group of women flagged down the bus. It was Grandma and my aunts. While the bus driver frothed, they gave Dad and us a sendoff I can still taste —a Malayali breakfast spread like no other: a feast on the roadside, featuring *dosas* (rice-lentil crepes), chicken curry, poached eggs, steamed yucca root, plantains with chutney, and, of course, coffee. Grandma clung to me and did not want me to go. I was always her *chutambi* (mischievous one). Dad hugged Grandma and kissed her on both cheeks. He hemmed and hawed over my aunts. Then, the four of us were on the road again.

***

A FEW MONTHS LATER, Dad advised Elisabeth to apply to medical colleges in Bombay and colleges in and out of state. John wrote disparagingly about CMC and discouraged Elisabeth from applying there. Naturally, this aroused Dad's suspicions. He advised Elisabeth to ignore John. Dad helped Elisabeth choose the well-established CMC over a new in-state medical college in Miraj near Bombay. After Elisabeth reached CMC, she could not avoid telling Dad about the goings-on. John had claimed he was doing an internship when, in reality, he was in his final year. It was shocking news, and Dad had hit the bull's eye again.

During his college years, including medical college, John's short stories appeared regularly in The Times of India, Indian Express, and The Illustrated Weekly of India. Although Dad fumed at them, he loved reading them and laughing his head off, as did we. The best was about Mario, a lovelorn Goan teenager, ditched by his Goan girlfriend, who wrote letters to her in a hopeless attempt to lure her back. John wrote book reviews for the Sunday Times. I remember he reviewed '*Sometimes a Great Notion*' by Ken Kesey, who later became famous with 'One Flew Over the Cuckoo's Nest'. Even though I silently cheered him on, it was terrible that John had stuck it to Dad. If only Dad had heard what John told me a few years later, he would be glad he finished medical college at all. In his third year, John told me he was one of two nationally selected candidates as a junior editor for the Times of India. He said letting go of that once-in-a-lifetime opportunity was an agonizing decision.

John and a classmate, Janaki, met Elisabeth at the railway station, and Elisabeth discovered that the two were more than classmates. Perhaps remembering the entitled Deshmukh, Dad was even more upset when Elisabeth told him that Janaki was a Hindu Brahmin. Interfaith marriages were unheard of and came with a steep price, with a lifetime of misery and discrimination awaiting the rule-breakers. Ma, sad but gritty like Grandma, supported Dad through this period.

Janaki grew up in East Africa. Her father worked as a railway guard for the British. After retirement, the now-wealthy pensioner and his family returned to India, and Janaki joined CMC in 1957, where she met John.

I was in ninth grade and rooted for John and Janaki. I looked forward to meeting her when she came to spend a few days with Nita in Bombay, a classmate whose father worked as an executive at an insurance company. Nita's two cousins, whom I shall call the Nayyar brothers, were distributors of steel slotted angles used in light construction. When the venture failed, they built multi-storied flats in Bombay's up-and-coming Juhu Church area close to the beach. I elaborate on the Nayyar brothers because they became notable characters in our lives after Dad's passing. John brought Janaki home to meet us, and she dazzled us all and hit it off right that first time. She complimented Ma on her delectable meals and how young Ma looked compared to what she had envisioned based on John's looks, which made him appear much older than he was. I observed a little wrinkle, though. She neither stepped into the kitchen nor offered Ma any help, although Ma, being in full Ma mode, would have hardly noticed these little inconsistencies.

They returned to college—Janaki to begin an internship in Pediatrics and John to finish his final year. Janaki then worked as a pediatric demonstrator and John went on to complete his internship, but did not return home; instead, he chose to stay at CMC and do nothing worthwhile.

In my letters, I pleaded with him to return and start a job, leaving space for Ma and Dad to plead some more. John ignored our pleas. Dad smoldered as the weeks became months. In a letter, John told me to mark my aerograms with a symbol on the front to show if anyone else was living with us. As his mole, I dutifully complied. In one letter, he warned Dad that he would not return until the coast was clear of guests, and I realized he was grasping at any excuse to delay his return.

A few weeks later, he asked me for help with his job search. I scoured the newspaper's classified section for jobs in Bombay for my errant brother. Meanwhile, whoever lived with us found a job and left, and Dad informed John. I sent a newspaper cutting for a Senior House Officer (SHO) position at GT Hospital in Bombay. We got a quick reply; he was on his way back. More than likely, he ran out of money. John started his first job as an SHO in the emergency room at GT.

The Wills cigarette incident happened after John's return home when I was 15, in my final year in high school. I hit a growth spurt and was just inches shorter than John. As his errand boy, I ran his cancer errands. Around this time, the much-ballyhooed taste-enhanced filter-tipped cigarette, Wills Navy Cut, appeared priced at over a rupee (100 *paisé* makes a rupee) for a ten-pack flat. The grocer mistakenly underpriced the new cigarettes from the outset, charging 30 or 40 paisé—an error of almost 70 percent. I told John about the windfall and dutifully returned the balance to him. After that first time, I took the exact amount to run his cigarette errand, a practice that lasted months.

The grocer finally caught on and demanded the money from me, and I told him John had it all. The grocer met John for the money, who feigned ignorance, which amounted to saying I had filched it all. I was speechless at how he shredded my character, throwing me, his brother, callously under those galloping horses. His lies and behavior, which I had often condoned, were now hurting me. The grocer's silent treatment of me never let me forget the incident. To top it all, I learned the meaning of being 'sucker-punched' when Dad laughed it off, told me what John had done to me, and warned me the world was crawling with them. I never did another errand for John.

Janaki returned for a quick civil marriage. Dad invited his best friend Joseph to witness the ceremony, and I attended as the only other family member. John sidelined Ma, saying they could not afford her presence. Volga Restaurant, located near Flora Fountain, held the ceremony and dinner. The restaurant's neon masthead with the name 'Volga' emblazoned with an artistic flair caught my eye, and the uniformed attendant with a bright-red jacket by the glass door reminded me of a lost member from the Queen's Brigade of Guards regiment.

John's choice of locale was impeccable. Mr. Gabardine was at his best. Janaki was beautiful and charming. They looked like models snatched from the pages of Femina Magazine. He was the 'know-it-all' and engaged the civil officer with his knowledge of the Volga River in Russia. He was skilled at small talk, often using it as a diversionary tactic. Only I knew he was gabardine through and through —too smooth to be real—unlike Dad's cotton. There were seven of us, including the officer and his clerk. I was surprised to be included on the guest list. I didn't care about the wedding, not as much as I did about eating at a posh, air-conditioned restaurant for the first time. I still feel guilty for not staying home, for Ma's sake. Ma hid her hurt without a complaint. Janaki's takeaway was that she could mistreat Ma without consequences.

It was dark inside; the menu was not easily discernible, but that did not matter, as it was a pre-set delectable meal with a slab of vanilla ice cream at the end. The ceremony was brief and unmemorable —an exchange of rings and a signing.

As we left Volga Restaurant hand-in-hand, Dad vented to Joseph a Malayalam truism: *'Naladhin oru cholè, alathdin oru thalè.'* The meaning is simple: 'If one cannot listen to good advice, one deserves a stinging slap across the bow.' It seemed like a throwaway line when his oldest had strayed away. Years later, I realized he deliberately expressed his sentiment with me by his side, within hearing range. Did he already realize the community's reaction would be harsh, not only to John and to his wife, but would embroil every member of the Daniel family as well? They would blame Dad, who failed to stop it with all his modern thinking. It had ended with what he rightly deserved. I heard all of it but ignored it as best as I could because his illness took over our lives within a couple of years. As Dad made the assertion, he glanced at me, and I tightened my grip in sympathy and reassurance.

Even though the Malayalam truism stayed in his mind, Dad's reservation about John marrying a Hindu Brahmin eroded as Janaki charmed her way in. Besides, her physical attributes were perhaps purposely on display. Her ill-fitting blouses and pronounced cleavage begged attention before Dad could observe the sheer beauty of her 1.618 golden-ratio face. It was the real deal—blemish-free, nicely sculpted nose and misty light brown eyes, all framed by silky black hair.

Soon after the visit, Janaki hurried to CMC and continued her pediatric job. When her parents heard about her civil union, they were apoplectic. To appease them, Janaki and John, along with his Sikh school friend Amrit, rushed to her village for a traditional Hindu wedding. During the three days of feast and fun with the naive villagers, John and Amrit arrived on white horses and underwent a face-saving sham Hindu marriage.

Janaki and John were home for good and became part of our joint family, an arrangement widespread in India. They took over Dad's bedroom and shunted him with his Kerala-made teak bed to the dining room corner.

Early on, Ma was quite accommodating to the changes Janaki wanted. However, it did not end there. Her Brahmin upbringing movie rolled frame-by-frame—affecting Ma and me. Janaki did not care whether she annoyed us or woke us up with the loud, off-key chanting of her *aarti* (devotional song), '*Om Jaya Jagdish Haré*,' a Hindu chant praying to the Lord of the Universe to bring prosperity and joy to the home. She sang the aarti while ironing her clothes at daybreak. She spewed all nine verses like an automaton. Coming from her, those well-meaning words meant nothing since her mistreatment of Ma following the aarti continued unabated. The whoosh of the hot iron, which followed every few lines of the chant as it went across the wetted cloth, was like a razor sharpening over a barber's strop.

Janaki was bright with impractical plans. Her idea to start a dispensary together meant that John would have to quit his job at GT Hospital. Initially, perhaps for months, no money would be coming in. From its hare-brained conception, it did not make sense, since two doctors were not necessary to examine one patient. Moreover, hospitals in Bombay were always looking for doctors. The project needed money, plenty of it, that Dad did not have. John's idea of borrowing from her well-off father got a resounding '*Nyet*.' The newlyweds argued bitterly over this.

They chose a place in the boondocks to keep costs low. Since it was a large loan, Dad's street-smart friend, Solomon, took him to a mobster, an Afghan *Pathan*. Until then, Dad only borrowed from friends, with no question of interest payments. Charging an exorbitant interest rate, the loan shark demanded timely payments. The tall, red-haired Pathan often stood across from the railway lines in the evenings and watched our bungalow, scaring the bejesus out of Ma. Dad borrowed against his better judgment, perhaps thinking he owed John for convincing him to pursue a career in medicine.

John and Janaki could not repay the loan, as they had assured Dad, because the dispensary hype did not pan out. Dad was stuck with the IOU, and would soon owe more than he borrowed. The dispensary earned a few rupees daily during its early months, but on some days, it earned nothing. Dad did not know or even suspect that the newlyweds had schemed to run the dispensary enterprise so they could schmooze together at work and play.

Meanwhile, the Marthomite uprising was revving up. Fame is a bitch. She unravels faster than a hooker, which isn't pretty to watch. It was no surprise that people began questioning Dad and Ma. You can only evade questions for so long. Dad and Ma could not lie or tell people to get lost. What were family secrets until then, namely John's marriage and his poor academic performance, became public and shocked the Marthomites. Many fretted that John's marriage was a harbinger of a trend and that their sons would break from tradition, ultimately destroying the community. It would perhaps be one of the first times in the community that someone like John dared cross that imaginary threshold by marrying a Hindu and marrying for love. The innuendos and rumors got wilder and more ridiculous. Some of it was attributable to Dad's nemeses, Fat Cherian and his cohorts. Dad's so-called forward-thinking and daily wanderings to the library and the hospitals happened while his oldest son had free rein. Some wished Dad had lost his right hand instead of his left. They were sure Dad's children (Elisabeth and me) would follow the trend. Then they picked on Dad and said his visits to hospitals to see the kids who had graduated from Sabita and B1 (2) were suspect, and he was doing all this behind his suffering wife. They even said he went to enjoy the nurses' company, even though they knew the nursing students were like his own daughters, relatives of his and Ma's, or good friends.

The accident was God's warning; they said there is fire where there is smoke. Water to quell these fires was nowhere near.

The truth ran away from us. Dad made sure RN trainees who had lived with us were under his watchful eye by visiting them. Dad was quick-witted; he likely joked with them and teased them. Dad made sure they studied hard, ate well, the hospital food they hated, attended church, stayed out of trouble, and, most importantly, sent some money from their stipend to their parents. He nipped stuff in the bud when they wandered off the trail. One example would be how Dad handled my wayward cousin's shocking behavior when she began dating an illiterate Malayali Muslim, a street vendor. Her brother quickly arranged for her to be married with a substantial dowry. Of course, Dad paid the price with the nasty letters he received, some perhaps demanding part of the niece's dowry, from her ingrate brother who stayed with us while job seeking, and was overseas among the sultans.

He did not have to worry about the boys, as he did the girls, who graduated from our home, because most of the boys had arranged marriages and usually received hefty dowries (illegal for namesake only) from the brides' families.

The next phase of our decline, ostracism, went viral. More heartache followed. People at church stopped talking to us, friends dropped off, and relatives seldom came by. Even Uncle George never came or helped us anymore.

⸺◉⸺

THE FOLLOWING YEAR, Dad had a prostate operation at KEM Government Hospital. The surgery went well, but the cleaning staff was on strike. His urine catheter and the urine collection flask remained uncleaned during his stay. I suspect this or another aspect of the surgery led to an infection that worked its way into his system.

⸺◉⸺

MATRON MARY WAS OUR only support. I visited her until I left India. Sadly, I lost touch with her. Matron Mary was the one person who did not judge John. Neither Uncle George nor Aunt Sara ever got over John's marriage. Uncle George came around a year after Dad's passing, but it was never the same. Aunt Sara was aloof, too. Aunt Sara became a big shot in the nursing field at the all-India level. She lived in New Delhi for a while, then moved to Calcutta (now Kolkata), where she worked as a teacher at the All India Institute of Hygiene & Public Health (AIIH & PH), the first such institution in the Southeast Asian region. She married late in life, and the couple stayed with us for a few days while visiting Uncle George. I stayed in touch with Aunt Sara during college and spent some holidays with her. Her husband joined us the first time I met her at the office, and we stopped by the famous Bentinck Street in Calcutta's Chinese shoe district on the way home. They bought me my first pair of handcrafted Beatle boots. They retired in the mid-1970s and returned to Kerala. I had already left India, and I lost touch with them. As Dad's dutiful son, I visited Uncle George whenever I went to India.

CHAPTER 10 PICTURES:

1. Family picture a few years after Dad's accident.
2. Grandpa and I after his misadventure with his haircut!

Chapter 11: Aftermath of a Death Sentence

My heart skipped a beat as the doctor's words coursed through our veins and knocked us about like pinballs on chemo. How Dr. Joshi kept on stabbing the elevator buttons made it seem he needed neurological help, too.

Waiting for him to vanish, I recollected our first meeting. We had entrusted my father's care to this neurologist extraordinaire, whose praises John sang to heaven. We believed John—neither pausing to consider his medical inexperience nor exercising Dad's lessons of due diligence and inquiry—which all were screaming code blue. Maybe it was more cultural than I had ever imagined, living as I was in a society where fealty towards its elders borders on mind-numbing insanity.

"We are lucky to get Joshi," John proclaimed. "He shouldn't even charge us." John was alluding to the long-standing tradition of doctors waiving fees when another doctor or an immediate family member was a patient.

Dad's illness started with a brief fainting spell at work, after which he took a few days off. Even though the weakness in his left leg and back pain worsened, they said, it was a vasovagal event. It gave John and Janaki an excuse to ignore Dad's complaints. His health went on a tailspin when the dispensary did not pan out. The loan shark invaded his thoughts. After each quickly consumed meal, he paced the veranda feverishly at night because he knew he would soon owe the mobster his soul.

Taking Dad to Elisabeth's Teaching Hospital was under consideration. It would incur expenses, and since he was drowning in debt, he asked two nephews for help. The two owed him big, but they refused—the first one, whom Dad put through college, denied ever receiving the letter. The second one (the gramophone cousin), whom he rescued after he ran away from his home in Kerala to work as a servant, and found him a factory training job and later a job in Kuwait, told Dad to get lost and advised him to borrow from John's in-laws. Oh boy, why didn't Dad think of that? Dad did not bother asking a third nephew, whose sister and he had also lived with us, and wrote Dad abusive letters. Dad may have sought help from others and realized the futility when his closest ones had ditched him. Saddled and saddened, Dad soldiered on.

Finally, John found the one Dad needed, hiding in plain sight—a famous neurosurgeon catering to patients privately and in a free hospital. Our first private visit with Joshi took place in the summer after I completed my SSCE. Dr. Joshi exceeded our expectations that day. After giving Dad a thorough checkup, he ordered tests at a lab he used and promised us a discount. While chatting with us, the doctor provided us with medicine samples and discussed John's future with him. When Dad managed to get a word in, he proudly informed the doctor that Elisabeth was a third-year medical student and his daughter-in-law was a doctor, too.

"Are you telling me you will soon have three doctors in the family? Incredible. I wish I had children like yours. That was a different time. India needs as many women doctors as male doctors. That baton is yours. Build a strong India and destroy the dowry system, sir," he advised freely. His accent was North Indian, probably from Punjab, a region known for its brave and hardworking people who had seen many marauding foreign invaders come and go, fleeing like Alexander or staying like the Mughals.

"I agree, doctor. Education is the best dowry I could give my daughter," affirmed Dad.

"That's the point," the doctor replied, "Provide the best education. You must also have smart children and enough in the bank, and you have both. Smart children and plenty of..." his voice trailed off. Then, with a mischievous twist of his lips, he rubbed his thumb and fingers together in the universal sign for moolah. I wondered if this was all about money since the doctor's camaraderie surprised Dad as it did me. I doubt Dad saw through it, even after what transpired next.

"You are rich, or you have a great job. Sir, where do you work?" asked the doctor.

Honestly, even at sixteen, I saw through his patronizing behavior. A trusting person like Dad was an easy mark, and he did not see through the double talk of diplomacy that had been cultivated through North India's long history with invaders. I don't recall him ever asking about Dad's noticeable handicap. Obviously, he was all about himself. Hesitantly, Dad replied that he was an officer in the Railways.

"Officer, officer, I knew it," the doctor repeated, beaming at Dad as he edged closer to me. He patted me and asked if I would follow my trailblazing siblings' example. A disinterested roll of the shoulders was all I could manage, my mind racing with the invading hordes as they ravaged the plains of North India. In any case, I considered his question presumptuous and premature. I was barely out of high school and had a ways to go. If the old buzzard had been a good friend, I would have slapped him back and told him to tone down. He was neither friend nor foe, not yet. All I saw were the attempts of the nimble-fingered Lakshmi, our peerless Hindu goddess of wealth, to pick Dad's pockets. I wondered how the doctor would react when she came up empty.

"Officer, officer... " Dr. Joshi repeated, revealing his gold-capped incisors. I was sure he knew about government jobs—title tall and salary short. Since Dad worked in the Claims Department evaluating claims for lost or damaged goods in transit through the BPT Railways, he had an opportunity for graft. Dad was straight as an arrow, incorruptible. All he got for his fair assessments was confectionery during *Diwali*, or *Ratnagiri Apoose* (Alphonso) mangos in the summer. After the visit, the doctor extended his hand for his fee and said, "Mr. Daniel, my charge is usually 200 rupees for a visit, but only 100 rupees from you."

Even though it was a considerable discount, Dad did not expect the doctor to blow off tradition. Besides, I was not sure Dad had any money, let alone a hundred. 'Are you going to charge this poor man?' I wanted to shout. Dad pulled out several crumpled 'just-in-case' ten-rupee notes from the hidden pocket Ma had sewn inside all his shirts, behind the front pocket, after a pickpocket had picked his front pocket soon after he went to work following the accident. I was sure that was all the money he had in the world. Dr. Joshi grabbed the ten-rupee notes John pulled out of his back pocket. Looking me over with a raised eyebrow for my contribution, the doctor thought the better of it and marched off.

Dr. Joshi could not contain his abruptness when he saw us again at the free hospital.

"Mr. Daniel? You should see me in my clinic, not here with so many to examine."

"I am not a rich man, sir. I can only see you in the government hospital."

A derisive snort escaped his lips, "For free checkups, you mean? You *Undgoondoos* are the same, and I cannot spend as much time with you as I usually do at the clinic."

'Undgoondoo' derogatorily described how the Dravidian words poured out from a South Indian in heavily accented torrents, rolling out freely as if there were no commas or full stops. Dad was broke after the previous month's visit.

His examination was swift. He ignored me, wrote some prescriptions, and dismissed us. It was all business with not even a hint of his earlier silkiness.

Dad's medications gave temporary relief, though his condition deteriorated. Years later, I found Dad's May 1965 lab report among the titbits in his green notebook. I may be mistaken, but the abnormal Cerebrospinal Fluid (CSF) results were extremely troubling. The lab results led perhaps to one conclusion: a bacterial infection. I tried to recall the medicines he took and came up with only pain relief medications throughout most of his illness. In light of his CSF readings, I would think that curing him would have been the priority. Was he too far gone, or was it too late to intervene for him to make his signature comeback? A few years later, in a moment of candor, John told us he and his wife should have done much more for Dad.

As we waited for the doctor to take the elevator, Dad searched my eyes to determine the extent of my understanding of the doctor's verdict. I gazed back steadily, eyes glistening from the light refracting through the large glass panels; I looked away and brushed off my tears.

"Look, son," he said as he held my chin lovingly, "Nothing will happen to me. No point in worrying others, especially your mother."

"Okay, Dad, but shouldn't John know what Joshi just said?"

"The good doctor was probably angry about something else. That's all. See where my left hand used to be. The pain now is nothing like the pain from the accident and the ghost pains. I'll be there for you, son, I promise."

I smiled back in disbelief, lips aquiver. Dad had ignored my question, and it seemed like he had decided that, regardless of my thoughts, it remained a matter between us, man to man. The promise he mentioned is what transpired at home a few months earlier. In April 1965, unexpected events occurred a week before my First Year of Science (FYSc) University exam, which did not help my studies. Ma rushed to Kerala for over a month to be with her ailing mother. Janaki ran the house, revealing more of her true self. Dad's older brother, whose son wrote nasty letters to Dad, showed up at B1 (2) after his family kicked him out of his home in Kerala and stayed with us for many weeks. Dad struggled without Ma and had to rely entirely on me. Dad's brother returned to Kerala six weeks later and died under suspicious conditions. I muddled through taking care of Dad and the exams and blew my first Indian Institute of Technology (IIT) Entrance Examination. I rationalized that I could redo it the following year. I passed FYSc with a second class. Although I was lucky to clear it, getting between 50 and 60 percent of the marks was unfamiliar territory. Around that time, John, familiar with what French architect Charles-Édouard Jeanneret (also known as Le Corbusier) had done with his master plans for the new city of Chandigarh in Punjab, which was close to the CMC, sold me on the idea of architecture.

Since I was so good at art, John pressured me to abandon IIT and choose Architecture instead. John was unrelenting, like the sparky character in 'The Caine Mutiny,' who egged others into doing his bidding. I halfheartedly completed my admission papers to the J.J. College of Architecture and submitted them before the deadline. Surprisingly, they put me on the waiting list and admitted me in late June 1965. Getting into the esteemed institution was a godsend, though it was not my first choice as a profession. Don't look a gift horse in the mouth was Mr. Gabardine's advice after he read my admission notice. I joined Architecture with the possibility of retaking the IIT exam. John's lack of confidence didn't bother me, although he knew better. I had beaten him in the benchmark SSCE, outperforming him significantly in Science and Mathematics with some perfect scores.

I knew I had made a blunder within the first few weeks of joining the architecture field. I realized I had always been a tinkerer and an engineer at heart. I cared little about the differences in bricklaying between English and Flemish bonds and other such mind-numbing subtleties. I discussed it with Dad, who advised me to give equal importance to both exams and clear both. Dad was confident I could pass both if I was diligent. Then, without any second-guessing, I would be free to choose between starting at one of the world's premier engineering institutions or continuing in Architecture as a second-year student. I lamented that I would lose a year if I passed both and pursued a career in engineering. He wisely advised me to record the lost year as an experience gained. His remark turned out to be prescient! Dad's help in resolving my dilemma of making the right decision was paramount. He swore he'd be there to help, just as he'd helped my siblings during such critical times.

As we struggled to the hospital's front door, his promise to help me was in jeopardy. Maybe my dreams would crash like a Sisyphean misadventure. I supported him as we labored towards the hospital exit, stopping as he leaned on me every few minutes. I searched his eyes to determine if their trademark sparkle had returned before I went to get a taxi.

I dreaded hailing cabs, especially near a busy hospital. Bombay taxi drivers are brusque. If you catch the eye of a passing taxi driver, you had better be ready to plead your case. Demand outstripped supply at busy spots, which meant that regardless of who came first, the taxi driver decided his next fare among the half a dozen applicants crowding around his windows. Among them were 'Romeos' whose hands wandered off, feeling the soft body parts of women. Pickpockets operated freely in such areas. His mighty gaze darted from face to face, selecting the finalist. Conversing in a mixture of Marathi and Hindi, he might even throw in a generous serving of epithets.

Bombay's notorious pot-holed streets are a minefield of debris. As I wandered farther from the hospital looking for a taxi, I deftly avoided a fresh mound of cow dung, only to slip on a banana peel. The feeling of zero gravity was luckily short-lived as I regained my foothold and continued my quest. I took a chance and darted into the passenger seat of an unoccupied cab. The cabby drove to the hospital entrance and helped me get Dad into the cab. The cab was clean, and a small fan churned the hot air without making much of a difference as Dad sweated profusely. A notice in the taxi stated that the driver had purchased the vehicle with a loan from the State Bank of India. Our poor cried out for unsecured loans to save India from its blights. Nobel laureate Muhammad Yunus scaled up the concept in Bangladesh, known famously as the *Grameen* approach. Next to the notice was a garlanded picture of Prophet Mohammed's First *Kalima* (aka Shahadat, the first of six pillars of Islam), the Muslim pillar of faith, which says, '*La Ilaha Illa Allah, Mahammmadur Rasul Ulla* (There is no god but Allah, and Mohammed is his messenger).' For India to succeed, that garland had to embrace every Indian regardless of caste, religion, gender, language, and creed.

The taxi honked and weaved its way to the station, dropping us at the pedestrian ramp bridge to the Sandhurst railway station (aka Sandas Road). The sandas moniker stuck because it was a filthy place. We climbed the ramp bridge, weaving through the crowds and avoiding the trash and red-tinged spittle around us.

Fortunately, the train arrived quickly, and as it rumbled to speed, the rush of air on our faces was a

welcome relief. As Dad dozed off with his sun-dazed head resting on my shoulder, I looked out the window, my thoughts confounded, unsure of what lay ahead.

When the train departed Sewri station, I stood by the boxcar's door, and Ma and I waved wildly at each other as I passed our bungalow. At Wadala, I helped Dad off the train as we gingerly retraced our way home. It seemed the rain was taking a respite. I was not looking forward to struggling with Dad on the shade less Reynolds Road. I dabbed his face with my handkerchief whenever we stopped to rest for a few minutes at people's doorsteps or leaned against lampposts. We passed the E, D, and C quarters, the dispensary, and finally reached the 'B' quarters.

Above the dispensary is where the doctor, whom I shall not name, lived with his family. He was a quack. The saying was that you went to him with a severe ailment only if you wanted him to hold your hand while you died.

As we turned the bend past the dispensary, Ma was there, peering through our front door. Dad placed a finger to his lips at our doorstep as he looked at me knowingly. I was unhappy that we hadn't accomplished a thing for all that toil. After we had Ma's fresh lemonade, I sat beside Dad, his head resting against me. Janaki and John worked in the mornings, came home for lunch and a snooze, and returned to work for a few hours in the evenings, and I wondered why they were not home yet.

With Janaki pregnant, her needs were foremost, and Dad's problems took a backseat. They were doctors in absentia, indifferent non-paying boarders in my father's house. John was at his backstabbing best and said Dad was faking it, clamoring for attention and competing with the unborn baby. All that Jung proved deadly.

The timepiece on the windowsill showed it was half past two, and Dad worriedly asked, "Are the children not back home yet?"

Ma was out of earshot in the kitchen and did not answer. I went to the kitchen to find out.

"What did the doctor say?" she inquired.

I ignored her question and asked, "Where did those rabbits go?"

"They said they would return after their evening shift at the dispensary.

"Ma, tell me," I asked, losing patience with her.

"They ate quickly and rushed off to Metro Cinema."

"Are you serious? You mean they are at a movie with Dad, so sick?" I asked, frustrated.

"I tried telling them, son. They said it was their last chance to see a picture show before the baby's arrival. They said they might stop by Joshi's and find out how it went."

Ma noticed my profound disappointment as she handed me the plates. They could join Joshi at his shindig for all I cared.

"Son, you ignored my question. Did something else happen?"

"Ma," I said, leaning against the door. "The doctor did not even take a good look at Dad."

As she stood there with her hand covering her mouth in disbelief, I told her how our visit had derailed.

"Dad cannot walk even slowly anymore, Ma. We were a few minutes late, but the doctor could have seen him. No medicine either, and it was a total waste."

"You left so early, too," she said, "Did you find out when he will see him next week?"

In my state of mind, I didn't even think about following up on his orders to his nurse. Tearing up, she searched my eyes, and her palms cupped my weary face.

"You are not telling me everything, are you?"

I broke down and felt foolish standing there bawling without an explanation. Ma knew something awful had transpired.

The food was hybrid today, like the hybrids we'd become.

Janaki's interference in household matters also affected Ma's cooking. Our daughter-in-law could

not cook worth a lick but dished out spades of snide comments about Ma's food, cooking, and even methods.

There was no peer to Ma when it came to Malayali cooking. Janaki's jabs had the desired effect, which got Ma to experiment. She would tell Ma to cut out critical ingredients like coconut from her *thorens* (fine-cut vegetable dishes) and curries. Ma's Malayali food went to hell. Her meals turned out to be neither North Indian nor South Indian. Our taste buds revolted every time she experimented.

That evening, Dad struggled to sleep after another mish-mashed meal. The matinée-goers returned late after work, anger writ large on their unsmiling faces; I guessed they'd been to Joshi's.

"How come you were so late?" they yelled at me, seemingly in unison.

"The task was simple enough. Take Dad to the hospital and see Joshi. We fixed the appointment. All you had to do was deliver Dad to the doctor, and you botched it royally, wasting everyone's time."

Their synchronized ambush robbed me of my voice, so I put my finger to my lips, miming that Dad was trying to sleep.

"Is that all you have to say? I messed up?" I whispered. "We were a few minutes late, and it's not like Joshi had left his office and gone to the races."

"The nurse said you were quite late," countered John. "You can't be late for these things. He is one busy man."

"Right! How come you didn't take Dad yourself?" I replied. "You are the bloody family doctors, aren't you? I could have accompanied Janaki to work while you took Dad to the hospital. You can still see only one patient at a time, right? Tell me, why do you need two doctors to see one patient? How come you went to a movie?"

I watched his filter-tipped cigarette quivering between his lips. I was not about to buckle like a deck of cards. I used to worship the ground he walked on. Over the years, I had peeled him, one overbearing layer after another. I unmasked his constant hassling and wisecracks for what they were: a coping mechanism. The final straw was the 'Wills' brand cigarette incident.

My unexpected response surprised them, Janaki especially. I nudged John through the door and out onto the street. My beef was not with the Brahmin, not yet, anyway. I stood under the lamppost, swaying, with my hands cocked at my hips. The light from the lamp above created a shadow effect on John's face, making him look surreal. He seemed startled by my posture.

"Do you have any idea what is going on?" I said. "It's easy to ambush me, but I will not let you do that anymore."

"I didn't mean to hurt your feelings," John replied. "He is our best hope, and we can't keep him waiting."

"Since when did you care about my feelings? That SOB is Dad's worst nightmare. Do you know what your 'best hope' told Dad today—do you?"

John was dumbfounded. Of course, he was clueless. Let him stew in the mire or pry Ma. All Ma knew was that something unspeakable had happened. My lips would stay sealed, and he would have to find out the hard way—ask Dad. I turned around and went back into the house. My kowtowing days were history, too.

Dad lay in bed trying to sleep, and did not get any better after that day. We tiptoed around him, wondering how to keep him from being so miserable. He did not read anything, did not bother with the newspaper headlines, and often asked me to lower the radio volume. As sick as he was, he had to have his morning bath. Before leaving for college, I bathed him. He enjoyed the last bit when I lifted the bucket and ran the rest of the water onto his head like a waterfall. After I wiped him off and helped him with his clothes, it was Ma's turn to do the rest as I got ready and rushed to college. All of this became too much for Ma when Dad's condition worsened. I tried attending classes sparsely so I could help Ma. I hoped Dad would recover, even if it were an incomplete recovery.

A few weeks later, on a Sunday morning, I listened to host Hamid Sayani and the Binaca Hit Parade on Radio Ceylon (now Sri

Lanka). While Dad sat listlessly picking at his breakfast, I went to the butcher on Kidwai Road. John and Janaki had already gone to their dispensary.

I rushed home to see how Dad was doing and heard him snoring. I relaxed and had another coffee as I read the Sunday newspaper. The front pages covered the previous week's skirmishes with Pakistan. I started on my books–Construction and Building.

Before long, I began gazing vacantly at the pages and soon dozed off. The aroma of spices in the meat curry woke me up. It awakened Dad. Soon, Ma would start making dosas. It's best to eat dosas while they're still hot. It was almost noon, and it was time for Dad's bath. Ma yelled from the kitchen that the hot water was ready. I helped him with his bath. I did all the talking since Dad was not in the mood. I told him about the friends I met at the class picnic and my impressive vocalization of Cliff Richard's songs. I exaggerated that three pretty girls, whom my classmates called the *'teen devian'* (the three goddesses) after a movie of the same name, even swooned as I sang. He may have cracked a faint smile, but I'm unsure, as my memory of that day has blurred. He perked up and asked whether I could sing for him after lunch. I said, "Sure, anything for a smile."

That year, Bollywood released Teen Devian (Three Goddesses), a hit Hindi movie. Dev Anand, the hero, was the poet who fell in love with Nanda, Kalpana, and Simi, the three famous actors of the time, in less than two and a half hours. Before its release, Teen Devian billboards sprouted everywhere in the city. Loudspeakers blared out the movie's songs. Although the three *'devian'* from my class were very different from the starlets on the silver screen, they were young and not bad looking. Tagging them with this moniker was inevitable because these shapely girls, with their hourglass figures, strutted together, joined at the hip. They were inseparable in class and throughout campus from my first day in architecture. However, for a faint smile that I observed, my once jovial Dad remained withdrawn after the hospital visit, and today was no different. He wanted to be alone with his thoughts.

Lunch was not ready, and I saw Ma vigorously grinding the chutney. It looked like we were in for a rare, simple, and great Malayali meal. As we sat at the table, Ma said she would wait for the 'children' to come so she could eat with them. I insisted that the three of us eat together immediately, and we did.

We dipped each dosa morsel in coconut chutney or sautéed potato-onion side dish and relished every bit. Then Ma brought in the steaming beef curry. It was indeed an unforgettable meal. Dad ate well that last time, and after I cleaned him up and eased him into bed, I lay on the sofa with a magazine. Ma rested on the other couch with the Sunday Times. Soon, my friend Shanti showed up for her afternoon chores.

Suddenly, everything fell apart when Dad started coughing and couldn't stop. Ma and I ran to his side. He threw up most of what he had eaten, all over himself and the bed. Ma and Shanti cleaned him up, and just as quickly, Dad passed out. I rushed to the front door to see if John and Janaki were in sight. Not seeing them, I dashed to get Dr. Death from his home at the dispensary. Holding the umbrella over the doctor in the pelting rain, I told him about Dad. He examined Dad and, finding nothing, told us to hurry Dad to the hospital.

Ma and Shanti got Dad ready, while I went to get a taxi. I darted across the rail lines through the gullies of the slums onto Kidwai Road, hailed a cab, and brought it home through the No.6 level crossing. There was still no sign of John and his missus. With the taxi driver's help, the four of us got Dad into the vehicle and rushed to the hospital. The staff admitted Dad to the neuro ward under the care of none other than my nemesis. John showed up a few hours later. Dad was still awake but completely exhausted. He finally fell asleep but looked at us before doing so, and without a word, he indicated that it was curtains. Ma burst into tears as Dad's stertorous breathing became too painful to watch.

The real work began soon after as I stopped classes and took full-time care of Dad for days on end. I brought breakfast and lunch from home, fed him as much as he wanted, and ate the remains. We didn't talk much, although I was lost in memories of our lives together as I sat beside him. Later, I made sure he ate the hospital-provided meal and went home.

One of the Residents even told me to take Dad home. Completely missing his import, I stammered that Dad was still not well. Later, it occurred to me that he was the neurosurgeon's errand boy. I wondered how often the underling had conveyed the attending's message. I recounted the incident to John, who went into denial, trying hard to dispel my forebodings. I wasn't having it. Soon, Joshi wanted to operate on Dad. My brother agreed, even though I thought it was a foolhardy experiment, given the Resident's request to take him home. In all likelihood, the doctor was stroking his ego with another brain surgery under his cap. After they shaved Dad's head, I could barely recognize Dad. The doctor assured us that brain surgery would be highly beneficial. The thing is, he did not tell us who it would benefit. As they wheeled Dad away, Ma and I kissed his forehead, and that was it. When he came out of surgery, he was in a coma. There was nothing to do but watch Dad day after day, asleep and unrecognizable. I held Dad's arm stub and gently massaged it for old times' sake to help with the phantom pains. I talked to him often, hoping he would wake up once. All the ugly now lay bare; he was so near yet hopelessly unreachable.

It was late Sunday evening, September 5, when Ma and I came from Dad's room and observed several knots of relatives and friends in the hallway. One giant knot in a far corner consisted of Dad's detractors and their lackeys joshing around. Uncle George went by, ignoring us, with two huge bags of oranges and apples. I knew it was showmanship because he knew Dad was still on a drip in a coma.

The surgery was the final straw. I felt cheated that I never talked to Dad again or said a proper goodbye. At 3 a.m. on September 6, Dad died with Ma, John, and me beside him. I watched John incredulously as he stood tall and assured Ma and me that he would care for us as a son and brother. Ma, young looking at 48, was now a widow. The hospital staff came to prepare his body for the morgue. Ma wanted nothing to do with Uncle George's oranges and apples and gave them all to the ward helpers. John and I left the hospital together, looking for a chai place around 4 a.m.

I cadged a few puffs from John as he chain-smoked. Sleepy heads occupying sidewalks groaned as storefront shutters stuttered open. In the only show of unity I can remember, we huddled over chai and had a somewhat one-sided conversation. Grappling with Dad's demise, I barely deciphered John's words, straining to hear. Let bygones be bygones. I nodded. We would soon get an eviction notice from BPT. Again, I nodded. Dad's pension was the only money coming to him. Really, I said to myself, that's Ma's, not yours. The disbursement would take time. He would have to pay *pugree* (illegal payment) to get a flat. The only way for BPT to speed up his pension was to stay in our railway quarters until release of the money. No one was there to help us—no Uncle George—maybe he would have to turn to Nita's dad. John's words confounded me. It dawned on me that Nita's dad would recommend his relatives, the Nayyar brothers, who were big fish in the bribery-riddled Bombay flat-building business. I was John's convenient sounding board. It should have jolted me to attention as I sat dumbstruck, watching his lips move. I wondered if he would do right by Ma. When we returned to the hospital, the staff had already taken Dad to the morgue.

The three of us left the hospital and reached home before sunrise. John freshened up and later met the undertakers to make the funeral arrangements. I did not see him until late in the afternoon. The undertakers brought Dad's body home in a simple wooden coffin with purple felt trimming on the outside and a gold-painted, thin sheet-metal cross and placed it in the center of our living room.

Sitting beside my father's coffin, I swallowed the tears that welled up, remembering the doctor as he cut down a vibrant man in his prime. The doctor delivered the warrant and went about his business with careless disregard. How many others had he hastened with his words and life-saving surgeries? Still, his effect on this ever-hopeful, ever-happy individual—my father—was unmistakable and unforgivable. Although I had no good reasons for being so down on the neurosurgeon, I would be remiss if I gave him an easy pass.

His body lay in full view, though his soul had fluttered away. This event in my life left an indelible mark on my mind. I was reeling for almost a month, worse off than I was after the accident. My wounds were so deep that hardly a day passed, even now, without thoughts of the craven death sentence and its aftermath. Looking back, I realize he afforded me the privilege of letting me into his life for a short while. My unwritten contract was now dead.

As the undertakers readied the casket, John asked the mourners if they would step out of the living room so the family could have some privacy with Dad. We entered the room and closed the living room door behind us. Murmuring people peered shamelessly through the windows and denied what we sought. I sat beside my father. I took a deep breath and quietly reached down to place a hastily scribbled note in his shirt pocket. I could not write down everything I wanted, but it would suffice. That note and Gandhi's acts of self-discipline chased me for the rest of my life, keeping me on the straight and narrow, keeping me from myself. As for singing, I sang every chance I got, to this day, even in languages besides English and Hindi, because it was tied to memories of Dad requesting a song from me and the two of them, Dad and Ma, clapping and cheering me on. I could not resist reaching under his vest and creeping deeper to feel his stubble, as I had done many times before. I searched for the semi-warm flesh one last time and was shocked at how ice-cold and distant it had become. The coldness passed into me as I held the familiar stub and sensed him talking to me.

He told me that even though he could not be around, I should give it my best and that I would prevail, 'be brave, heed Ma, and take care of her.' He said he could see the note I was writing and knew I meant every word. He tried to fight back, but this unseen enemy had other plans. I finally let go and turned towards the door that led to John's bedroom, getting away from the smell of death, the stifling fragrance of lilies, and the cheap cologne.

His absence became a looming presence. I saw him everywhere. The catharsis of grief affected me differently. Perhaps I should have cried, but I just couldn't. I was monosyllabic for months, hurt beyond hurt, and clueless about what was coming next. I did not have to wait long.

My father's accident, his premature passing, and my brush with death were the three main events in my life. They were so all consuming that no light of reason could enter—nothing in me would let go of them. I have thought about my escape from the train many times and still see and hear the screaming, faceless faces who gave me a chance to live. As I navigated through life's problems, I often wondered whether it would have been better if I had died that day. I realize there is no answer to such speculation. There was no turning back; I had to hang tough, alone, and prevail.

⸻⬤⸻

CHAPTER 11 DOCUMENT: May 1965 Lab report.

The Cerebrospinal Fluid (CSF) Analysis was abnormal. The fluid is typically clear, but in Dad's case, it was turbid and showed 'plenty' of pus cells (dead cells). Dad's medications were mainly palliative from the outset. It was untenable, given that we had three physicians within striking distance!

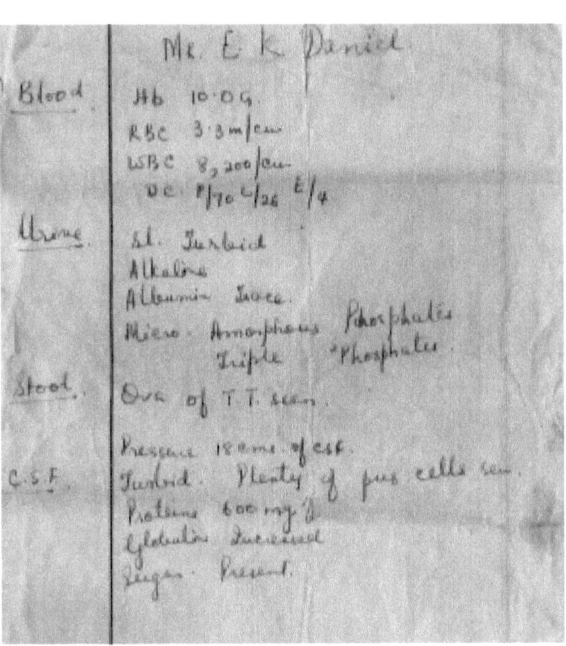

Chapter 12: Billiards with Best Friends

I met unexpected resistance when I pushed to open the door. It yielded, and I stumbled into Narendra Kumar, Nanda for short, my best friend. All my friends, whom I considered my brothers, were there. They put on a brave front—Nanda's older brother Raj Kumar, Vijay Karnik, and Bhaskar, all Hindus, along with Sydney Lobo, a Goan Catholic, Ashraf, a Muslim, and Jacob, a Jew.

Bhaskar lived in the servants' quarters close to our bungalow. He was two grades below me, although he was a few years older than I was. Being a Dalit, I realize now that he did not get a chance to start school on time like the rest of us. The others were a grade below me. I looked at all their sad faces and gulped. Bhaskar, who was always rock-solid, looked bleak. They knew I would have to vacate the quarters soon. Bhaskar said, "Hey Mathew, what do we do now? How soon will you be leaving us? Your Dad was such a gentleman. He talked to me often."

Coming from him meant everything to me, and I thanked him. Dad talked to Bhaskar, asked him about his studies, advised him to clear his SSCE, and even assured him he would find him a good job when he finished school.

"Whatever it is, wherever you move to, we will come to see you every week, I promise," said Nanda, coming out with one of his usual hyperboles.

"Listen, *chammars* [cobblers], we are not leaving that soon. We don't know when or where we'll move," I said.

With my sorrow buried deep inside, bottled up, I hugged each other. I had known Nanda, Kumar, Vijay, and Bhaskar since we moved from Dadar when I was nine. I had known Sydney, Ashraf, and Jacob for nearly six years since they moved to the new high-rise quarters built behind the D and E quarters. Vijay lived above us in B1 (3), and the brothers lived in a ground floor flat in the four-story building behind our bungalow. Regardless of our diverse backgrounds, we were brothers brought together by our proximity in location and age and a common purpose of playing together, mainly cricket, every chance we got.

Despite the crowd, my mind flashed back to bits and pieces of this place, which were bits and pieces of me. Before becoming bedridden, Dad walked on the veranda before his evening bath. When I was younger, I walked behind him, imitating his gait, singing our national anthem, and saluting with a turn of my head as we passed the front door. The fifty-foot veranda had also served as my beloved cricket pitch, where I bowled my tennis ball or the hard and heavy field hockey ball at the stumps charcoaled at the center of the north wall. Seemingly alive though immovable, they witnessed my tireless bowling and recorded the many times I missed them.

I appealed to the wickets as if they were umpires, imitating the big-name cricketers, cajoling them into declaring an out. After each good ball, I demanded their verdict by shouting, "Howzat [How about that]?"

They screamed back, telling me to do a better job, yelling and shaking their tops, "No way it's out.

The ball should hit us or the bails when we call an out, little master."

"You know, there's more than one way you can call an out, right?"

"That's right, little master, we understand, but..."

"What?" I cried in exasperation. "You've got to watch me and to whom I am bowling the ball. Like Roy Gilchrist, I bowl pacers to sloth-like batters. I rattle them and get into their heads. I bowl spinners and googlies like Richie Benaud to flashy Hanif

Mohammed or Abbas Ali Baig and bore them to tears. Do you know that googlies spin in the opposite direction to the expected direction, confounding the batter? Subhas Gupte was good at that. I am not trying to uproot the wickets because if I bowled down the line, they would smash every ball the length of Reynolds Road. I am trying to get them to lash out and make mistakes, such as a hit-wicket, catch, LBW, run-out, or whatever. There! You've got to imagine and give me an out for trying to entice them," I patiently explained.

"We are trying, little master. We don't even know your jargon."

"What, do you mean... trying... and jargon? Hit wicket is easy enough—the bat hits the wickets by mistake, and it is out. So is LBW. 'Leg before wicket' is as plain as a plate of rice... the batsman's leg obstructs the ball from hitting a wicket. So is run-out—you are out while trying to run between the wickets. These are all outs. Never mind, dear wickets, all three of you irritate me."

"Little master, how do we call something we cannot see, feel, or imagine?"

"Stop it, will you? Stop calling me little master."

My appeals to them were always for naught, especially when even Elisabeth, sometimes my play-by-play commentator, derided me, cast a wry eye, and always sided with the stumps. I sucked it all up, bowling the ball tirelessly and doing my best. Even though she teased me as the idiot who could not bowl straight, she had changed her old ways after John, my main tormentor, left for medical college.

⸺●⸺

TRUE TO FORM, IN 2007, on a visit to see Elisabeth, she told me I was a 'nothing' as we were leaving her house on a bright morning. Soon after, a letter came from her that I finally read in 2022, so I could mention it in my memoir. She complimented my Mughlai biriyani for her party the evening before I became a 'nothing.' Nary an apology, nothing about 'nothing,' either. A few years earlier, after

Ma's passing, she had written a letter telling me how much Ma loved me, how I kept her in stitches, and most importantly, how much better I was to Dad and Ma than they, meaning John and her. I was deeply stung by the 'nothing' title I earned for nothing. Hurt though I was, I resolved she would never again have her 'bhaiya, the milkman,' for breakfast.

———◦———

"MATHEW, I'M SORRY, we didn't know he was so ill. What will we do?" asked Nanda, echoing Bhaskar and breaking my reverie. The question was a loaded one. Our table tennis (TT) games and cricket would be the first to go. Being good at cricket was no fluke because I always practiced on the veranda. As for TT, I even took on adults at the club and gave them stiff competition. My prowess at these games was a secret at the big school because no classmate knew how much I played with my homies. Classmates living near the big school had no problem playing for an hour before school started. Besides the time it took to get Dad and me ready, living far away took me nearly forty minutes to an hour to reach school. I barely made it to school on time, usually making it as the national anthem wound down before First Bell at 10 a.m. Although my classmates played cricket during the lunch break, I didn't care to do so in the midday heat, as I would be sweaty and stinky all afternoon. Besides, I was neither a mad dog nor an Englishman. I kept up my façade as an elocutionist and a scholar, not a jock. I hurried home after school because my friends, who attended nearby schools, were waiting for their captain to arrive.

I whispered, "Nanda, listen, he is not hurting anymore. That's all I wanted for him at the end." Looking at Nanda standing there, sad like the others, I wondered whether we could ever be carefree again. We had been on so many adventures and capers together. We still had eggs on our faces from some; others remained jewels forever. The one we crowed about most happened at the Reynolds Clubhouse when I was 13. Billiards at the club was for older kids and adults. Besides, one had to pay to play—money we paupers never had. It would not have been a big deal if the billiards table had been lousy. This was a full-sized imperial billiards table in all its splendor, our clubhouse's jewel, a table even India's famous 1958 billiards amateur world champion, Wilson Jones, would have been proud to play on. It never stopped beckoning us, teasing us silly. It gnawed at us until we could no longer stand it. One day, we hatched a plan. We would break into the clubhouse and play billiards when the caretaker closed it for the afternoon. It became our crowning caper for the wrong reasons.

On the morning of the big day, we set off the trap by halfway 'unlatching' one of the billiards room doors. The caretaker usually inspected the latches from afar. We figured he'd miss it, which he did. We watched him head back to his quarters at noon. Soon after, we went home for lunch as well. I stuffed my pockets with everything I thought we needed for an afternoon of uninterrupted billiards. Then we triggered our caper.

Nanda tugged at the billiards room door, which opened willingly, and we were in as planned. We turned on the lights in the room, and the billiards table's rich green felt smiled at us. We planned to use the cue balls the caretaker kept in a cupboard, which he often forgot to lock. We were disappointed seeing the locked cabinet; breaking its latch with our bare hands was impossible.

I said, "Look what I have," producing four semi-fuzzy tennis balls from the pockets of my baggy shorts. We cued the balls on the table. Kumar took the first shot as Nanda and I stood by, chalking our cues like pros. We pretended to be smoking and flicking the ash onto the felt, a definite No-No. We played two rounds and were well into our third when we heard a latch sliding on the door to the large room—the one I had overlooked. I pocketed the balls. In a panic, Nanda switched off the lights. That was brilliant, Narendra, simply brilliant. We rushed to the door, blinded by the sudden darkness, and stood paralyzed, unsure of what to do.

Raj headed for the door to escape without us when he suddenly looked back and stopped short upon realizing he would be going 'coward' on us. The thought of surrender never crossed my mind, and I would not give up without trying. Like Arjuna, the Mahabharata's ace-archer who, when he aimed, saw only the reflected eye of the wooden fish in the water, I had to focus on the latch and think only of escape. Nanda and Kumar pushed against the door with both hands while I tried to latch the bolt with one hand and resist with the other. The latch wavered around the hole as I tried hard to slip it in countless times, and I felt my concentration waning and time slipping away. The caretaker, wondering at the stuck door, pushed hard from his side as we silently resisted. The fellow was a short, muscle-bound brute, but we were two and one-half strong as our struggle continued, and I kept fumbling and missing the hole. The excruciating suspense did not let up. When I thought I could not hold it together any longer, with sweat pouring down my face and my head drained of all blood from looking up for so long and about to faint, the bolt slipped in. The caretaker heard the sound and finally realized someone was on the other side of the door. He banged on the door and cursed.

We sped through the entrance and took off without anyone seeing us. Phew, that was close! Later that evening, we returned to our crime scene only to find the caretaker fibbing about the thieves he braved to save the club. We settled for TT, badminton, and cricket, knowing we almost had billiards all summer, too. Over the remaining holidays, we spent much time egging on the caretaker, who spun more stories of his brush with the bandits.

Great memories and great times with great friends; Dad's untimely passing would end them all. Things I took for granted now seemed so precious. I remember leading my friends up Mr. Chitnis's rooftop to steal his prized mangoes, fearlessly risking a two-story fall. We rented bicycles, and I led the breakneck 15-mile charge through dangerous traffic across the Mahim Causeway to Juhu Beach and back. We would never again, as a team, leave restaurants without paying the bill, having always ensured that we left a small tip for the waiter as a token of our appreciation for his cooperation. There would be no more crashing weddings at the Parsi Colony Hall, embarrassing the bridegroom by asking him if he was ready to go out with us that night and play Matka (an illegal numbers game) before his flustered bride. There would not be any more exciting days, one after the other, one caper after another, one cricket game after another, and one club visit after another. In short, life as I knew it had ended. There would be no more living.

I moved away from my friends and met my distraught relatives. After the hearse's arrival, the undertakers were ready to transport the coffin, and John and one of our relatives assisted them in carrying Dad's casket. The undertaker took pictures, hurried to set up one last shot, and positioned John, Ma, and me around the open casket, surrounded by relatives. I could not take my eyes off Dad as he clicked. I stared at Dad, the sunlight bathing his face for one last time. With his shaven head, he was barely recognizable. I finally looked away, not ready to break down. There were too many people waiting to see us falter.

The undertakers nailed the coffin shut and shoved it into the hearse. They did a final sweep of the bungalow, gathering all the wreaths, garlands, and flowers and throwing them around the coffin. They closed the double doors to the hearse. Ma and I got into the car right behind the hearse. I looked around for John and asked Ma where he was, and she told me that he had left to see Janaki in the hospital. I had no qualms about his departure since Janaki was due imminently, but he could have told me. While people speculated about missing John and his Hindu wife, hardly anyone knew she was due to give birth any day.

Sewri Cemetery was over a mile away, and most mourners walked to the burial grounds. There was an official-looking car behind us, and Ma said it was Mr. Madhavan, the mayor of Bombay. I squinted to see if I could make him out, and sure enough, there was Uncle Madhavan. I had met him several times when he visited our Dadar tenement to see Dad. His Honor, a Hindu from Kerala, was Dad's friend and protégé. He came to Bombay a few years after Dad. Long before becoming mayor, Dad called him Bombay's first citizen because he was an officer in the Bombay Municipality and on his way up. When he became mayor, Bombay's population was more than four million. Madhavan, renowned for his charitable work throughout his long career, received a well-deserved appointment. I wish I had paid more attention to their conversations. However, he was one of many who came to see Dad. Sometimes, I would hang around, letting on that they had outstayed their welcome. When that didn't work, I went out to find friends for a game of "inspectors and robbers."

After I started Montessori and suddenly became aware of girls with pigtails, I invited Prema's daughter, Vijaya, to join us. She was at least a year younger, a bit too young for my liking. I usually made Vijaya the robber, trying to steal our possessions as Chinka and I lay asleep on the floor. Chinka and I used to sneak peeks up Vijaya's petticoat since she never wore underwear and marveled at her mons Venus. The good thing about having Vijaya play with us was that she occasionally brought Kamala, Sawant sahib's daughter, along. Kamala was a bit bossy and a few months older than I was. I wondered what Kamala looked like. She was stylish, a prim and proper lotus always in lace-trimmed cotton pastels and, unfortunately, underwear. Kamala was the rich kid on the block, out of place among the urchins. I looked forward to Kamala being my fellow inspector because she was neat and organized and was the only grown-up among us, ensuring equal turns. Most importantly, I often held her soft hand as we searched for the daring thieves and the missing 'Kohinoor.' Hand-in-hand, we scoured the dangerous make-believe world as I squeezed her hand, and she did the same, turning my face red for no apparent reason.

These memories raced by as I watched Madhavan. He took time from his mayoral duties to pay his last respects, which demonstrated his genuine care. He would miss Dad's counsel, and his presence at Dad's funeral turned many heads. Although he had not visited us since we moved to the remote suburbs, I am sure he and Dad kept in touch.

The hearse charged ahead of us. It was a relic from the British occupation, and I am sure it had seen better days. It moved well above the 20-kph speed limit on worn-out leaf springs. In 1965, Reynolds Road rarely saw vehicular traffic. I only hoped the hearse would make it to the pearly gates.

Our procession, stretching far, stopped at the railway crossing for the Harbour Line trains to pass. The gatekeeper opened both gates and waved us through. The hearse jumped the track protrusions and sped away. I saw Dad's coffin jump several inches, sending the wreaths and bouquets flying. I was sure Dad was suffocating as I watched helplessly, thinking about Dad's last rattling trip to his own funeral. By the time Ma and I reached the cemetery, the casket had been unloaded and moved to the gravesite. An even bigger crowd awaited us. Mayor Madhavan came by and offered his condolences to Ma. Our church pastor did the same. Ma looked lovely and fragile in her white sari and blouse while Amini, Ma's niece, stood by, dabbing Ma's tears and her own. Cousin Amini from Palai, Kerala, stayed with us while job-hunting. She was great fun and used to put on Dad's clothes and my hat, carry an umbrella, and prance around in a near-perfect imitation of Charlie Chaplin and Raj Kapoor. We dressed up as the siblings Hansel and Gretel. She dressed as our haggard dad, and we begged for alms in heart-rending Malayalam. We wanted Amini to stay with us forever, but Dad found her a position as an RN trainee.

I held Ma's hand, frequently reassuring her everything would be fine, even though I had a sinking feeling. Beyond our turmoil, India and Pakistan edged into an ill-advised war the day my father died. After living through WW II, Ma knew how war and misery belonged together. Ma told me more than once that Dad no longer had such worries. The sadness on many people's faces was all-pervading. To many, he was a person who had guided and helped them, giving them his all.

Amidst the lament and the muffled sounds of grief, Fat Cherian caused a commotion. I watched as he plowed through to the first circle of mourners around Dad's coffin and pelted the coffin with dirt. Eager to be the first to send off Dad, he slipped and almost joined Dad in the pit. About to giggle, I returned to my graveside manners when I felt a gentle nudge from Amini.

Then, the skies opened up with the casket still not fully covered, bringing an unseasonal downpour, short and heavy. While the crowd scampered to the nearby trees, we three—Amini, Ma, and I—stood there, thoroughly soaked. At least for a few minutes, Dad ensured the privacy we wanted. Dad's burial was on the same day he died—September 6, 1965. He was 52. On September 7, Elisabeth arrived home too late for the funeral. Later that day, Ankita, Dad's first granddaughter, was born to Janaki and John. Though my father's suffering was over, I sensed ours was beginning. Were these setbacks ever going to stop, or were we fated to lurch from one to the next? What was the fearless one to do with all this fear? Was this how my father's house would end?

The answers were brutal and quick.

CHAPTER 12 PICTURE: Best friends

1. Standing: Holding cricket bats, with arms around each other's shoulders, Bhaskar on my left.

2. Kneeling: Nanda second from right, Vijay to his right.

Chapter 13: Breaking Free

India was at war, and Bombay stood in shock as emergency measures took effect. They turned off the streetlights, and essential traffic crawled without headlights. People were panicky after air raid sirens went off at whim, freaking everyone out. Flag-waving precinct wardens and their lackeys walked up and down Reynolds Road, whipping up fear, shouting to cover windows, and warning that bombing by Pakistan's American jet fighters was imminent. We knew we were all sitting ducks without any shelters if the jets did come.

Dad's good friend, who'd helped me with Marathi during my school years, met me on the local train a few days after Dad's passing, and, sitting opposite me, he asked me kindly whether Dad's death was due to my brother's marriage. Shocked by his well-meaning insensitivity, I was unwilling to accept the question's premise. I looked him in the eye, hurt, as I whispered with a weak 'no' and turned away, not saying another word for the rest of the trip. People with question marks for eyes were all around me, and I faced them with a brave front while I raged within.

Our bereavement never got off the ground as improbable events quickly buried us. Janaki's parents lived near the War Zone. Fearing for their safety, she dispatched John to bring them home. John's promises at Dad's bedside were in limbo. Ma continually prayed for their safe homecoming. As the new man of the house (ha, ha), I brought Janaki and Ankita home from the hospital. The baby was feverish and cranky. Janaki was ready to try anything to bring down Ankita's raging fever after allopathy failed. I ran that night to the homeopathic clinic, miles away. I made it before it closed, and as I ran back with the medicine, I remembered my thoughts as I held Ankita for the first time: how swiftly one life replaced another. I cried aloud as I ran through dark streets, thinking of her and Dad, "Dammit, don't take her too." The homeopathic meds didn't help. Resigned and fearing the worst, we took turns cooling her down. Finally, the fever broke, and we burst out laughing as her listlessness gave way to bouncy baby wiggles.

John and his in-laws arrived a few days later, tired and frayed after their three-day trip from the front. John, hot around the collar, seemed worse for wear. The old couple must have slowed him down with the many bags they insisted on bringing. Ma, eyes puffy and sad, bravely greeted them with a warm smile and refreshment. They ate some of it and drank the chai hesitantly, without comment. We attributed it to their unfamiliarity with South Indian food.

Soon the horrors of Brahmin customs steamrolled us.

Ma readied a room for them, but they would not have it. Instead, they settled down on the veranda facing the street with bedding and belongings. The old couple shunned Ma's kitchen, along with her utensils, and decided to start a *rasoi* (kitchen) on the veranda for all to see, occupying half of my cricket pitch. Everything in our house was *joota* (contaminated). My study desk on the veranda got the boot to accommodate their kitchen. My stumps, etched next to my desk on the wall, suffered silently. As the insults piled, Janaki naturally sided with her parents instead of being a voice of reason. John played dumb and 'vassaled' along. Ma let it all slide, thinking the three would come to their senses. Hold on, Ma, do you mean to say the senseless can become sensible? I was appalled because none of this made any sense. We became outcastes in our home.

The curmudgeonly Mr. Shorey, an avowed vegetarian, made a shocking request. He asked Janaki if Ma could let him taste her non-vegetarian dishes—Ma's meat curries and fried pomfrets (a tasty fish from the Perciform family) were what he was after. Ma complied.

He demanded more, including Ma's potato stew and vegetable thorens. I suppose he was affording Ma the privilege of feeding a Brahmin, ha! The nonsense they piled on us as if we were such trash to live with was a sick joke — hypocrisy brewed in humiliation and hate under the cover of religion.

Janaki only worsened after her parents' departure two and a half months later. She snapped broom handles over her doubled-over knee with hate. Her piercing eyes and sharp tongue were like glass shards, cutting and flaying us. Like a clever kite roaming the Bombay skies, Janaki hid her talons, rode the currents of conflicts, picked the one that pleased her most, and then tore into us, Ma especially.

She was the quintessential quidnunc—a meddling Medici, as she galloped roughshod into my mother's business. She took on the role of the thespian Lalita Pawar, the conniving, mean mother-in-law of many a Hindi movie. I thought Pawar and her ilk would have gone out like the silent talkie in my new India. However, the mythical mean mother-in-law of Indian folklore reversed in my sister-in-law's persona. When Janaki shockingly mocked Ma, saying her heart was uglier than her face, Ma looked at me, closed her eyes, and shook her head, stopping any comeback from me—a classic 'turn the other cheek' learning moment for me.

After such instances, Ma often withdrew into her cocoon as I consoled her. John even called his wife Hitler and other names, followed by his hollow 'deep-in-the-bowels' snigger, but she had already reeled him in with her diktats. She had turned into a Delilah to my brother's milquetoast.

Seeing how tenuous my life had become in just a few months, I was desperate to abandon my dreams and move on. One hot and sultry day, in a fit of frustration, I went to the recruitment office of the Indian Air Force in Marine Lines, knowing well my enlistment would hurt Ma to no end. Finally, racked with conflict, common sense prevailed, and I fled when they called my name. I joined my compatriots on the sidewalk, a microcosm of my India. I rubbed shoulders with people from everywhere. I waded through the sounds, the smells, and the cacophony of their pitter-patter, laughter, and patois. Drenched in sweat, I felt like I was dowsing blindly with a forked twig, seeking signs of water. I realized I was rushing to my tenement roots—to an inevitable destination—Dadar. My nostalgia for the dreadful place, still miles away, startled me. I had lived an innocent life there, with diversity itself—Brahmins, other Hindus, Dalits, Muslims, and Christians. Memories of my happy existence there played out as I continued to trek on.

Hours later, I saw Sabita building looming ahead. Exhausted and feverish from the heat and exercise, I sank into a chair in a nearby chai shop. I could barely see those windows that had opened my young eyes and made me master of all I surveyed. I recalled saying goodbye to my father from those windows on the day of the accident that turned our world upside down. After having tea and Gluco biscuits, I stepped out of the shop. Then, my life changed forever when I ran into Otta Kaiyan.

"Hello, Otta Kaiyan. How are you, sir?" I burst out.

Initially, OK seemed baffled by the familiarity, and there was no way he could recognize me after our last meeting when I was a smart-aleck seven-year-old. Then, he completely floored me in fluent Malayalam.

"Yes, I am an Otta Kaiyan. I am Abdul Rafi from Kasaragod, a Musulman [Muslim], and a Malayali like you," he said.

Stunned speechless, OK continued about Kasaragod, his Kerala hometown, which had a sizeable Muslim population. As a Malayali, he most likely understood the moniker I had jabbed at him from my window. Staring at him, I saw not the scary face from my childhood but a disfigured Picasso-like rendition of a handsome face, one of a man who had weathered many storms. Everything about him was a story. His drooping left eye told a story. His scar-ridden face said another. His hapless attire was a third and his missing hand one more. He was a book of sad but brave chapters, filled with endurance, resilience, and hope. I had shed my childhood tears for him and even convulsed at every blow he took.

Tongue-tied initially, I hesitantly spoke, "Will you forgive me, Otta Kaiyan, sir? I always thought you were from the north. Forgive me, Otta Kaiyan, sorry, Abdulji."

Abdul stared past me. As I held my gaze, I saw his eyes crackling alive. Brushing away my question with a wave of his hand, he exclaimed in Malayalam, "What are you saying? What is there to forgive? I am a useless Otta Kaiyan."

Having established his credibility by speaking in Malayalam, he switched to a mixture of Hindi and Marathi. He had mastered them over the years he lived in Bombay, of which he lived in Dadar all the nine years I had seen and had obliquely known him. The gist of what he recounted was this: A year before finishing high school, he ran away to Bombay in search of work. He was the first in his family of several children to reach high school and was quite fluent in Malayalam and English. He sought adventure, not fieldwork. He always regretted not finishing his final school year. He arrived in Bombay via Bangalore from Kasaragod during the mid-1930s. He found a job in Dadar at a printing press. Since he knew English, he found work as an assistant typesetter. He also learned the ropes of binding books, the shop's side business.

Sawant, who became the kingpin, had also found his first job as a helper at Abdul's printing shop. They became friends, and Abdul took him under his wing. Sawant, a village kid from the Presidency of Bombay (known as Maharashtra State since 1950), ran away to the city seeking his fortune. Sawant did not see himself in the printing business. He was young, brash, impatient, and less educated than Abdul Rafi, and he got involved in 'get-rich-quick' schemes. Two years later, Abdul had an accident at the printing shop and chopped some of his right-hand fingers while operating the binder's guillotine. He was careless in taking care of his injury, which became infected. He underwent a total amputation of his arm to arrest the infection. Abdul Rafi lost his job and any means of livelihood. Sawant took care of him as much as he could. His destitution led to his eviction, and his neighbors petitioned the owner to let him stay in the building. Thus, the stairwell became his home.

Prohibition was in force, and Sawant became a full-time bootlegger. He could not spare much time for Abdul. Transporting *bewda* (moonshine) made under unhygienic conditions was the norm. Sawant became feared and ruthless in the underworld and diversified into other daring activities, such as protecting neighborhood businesses and Matka. As his businesses grew, he saw little of his friend Abdul. He ruled our neighborhood with ruthlessness and guile, maintaining his 'leader' façade by avoiding contact with Abdul. They did not talk much, but Sawant would spare a fiver or two for his friend when their paths crossed.

The story rang true. It all made sense now, especially Sawant sahib's protective behavior towards Otta Kaiyan. Whenever the tomfoolery directed at him got mean-spirited, Sawant stopped it. I felt we were kindred puppets on a leash. After all, he was someone I had rooted for, someone I had shed my childhood tears for, and someone who inspired me. Like Dad, Otta Kaiyan came from Kerala in search of work and worked for only a few years before becoming destitute. Dad worked for many years before losing his arm. These similarities were eerie. When Dad was home recuperating, I vividly remember how, upon spotting Abdul Rafi, I hollered, "Otta Kaiyan is here..." Those words hurled with scant regard slipped out of me before I stopped abruptly upon realizing my Dad was also one-handed now. This new reality hit home hard. Thoughtlessly, the words that slipped from my lips when I greeted Abdul were 'Otta Kaiyan.'

I trudged all those miles to find inspiration in my old neighborhood and walked right into the unlikeliest of all to provide it. I recounted my story to Abdul, from Dad's accident to his premature death, the aftermath, and my reasons for wanting out. I lost all composure when I finished, and so did he. That is when his eyes became fully alive and engaged with mine. Suddenly, there was a flashback in his mind as he recalled greeting a man returning home from the hospital after losing his arm. He now connected the man and me—Dad and me.

"Hey, kid, please don't cry. I swear I will find you a place to stay in my building. I know a kind Brahmin woman there, and I will ask Sawant sahib about a job, too."

That was all I needed. My face fell at the prospect of another Brahmin in my life. When I told him why I was sad, he dispelled my worries and pleaded with me to try it. It was as good a place as any to explore our shared humanity. Take a chance, start my comeback, my inner voice whispered. I discerned a faint light at the end of a grueling journey. Realizing there was so much at stake if I failed to act, I told him to go ahead and do the needful. The Indian Air Force would have to wait.

Immersing myself in my studies could become a reality again. My parents had laid the groundwork and instilled in me the need to better myself, and the fierce urgency of 'now' consumed me. To excel in both exams, I had to immerse myself in the subjects, now: trigonometry, calculus, geometry, physics, chemistry, sociology, architectural history, building and construction, and architectural design. I had to concentrate and transcend to a higher level now. I had to leave home now. I had to do what Dad did by leaving home when he did, NOW.

I never imagined it would come to this, never imagined fleeing home. Running out of time, I decided to go after what mattered—my struggle for relevance and my battle to save my father's house. Although I stood up for Ma, my presence and obduracy made it worse, and I rationalized that my absence would have the opposite effect.

Ma and I talked well into the night about my encounter with Abdul. I made her understand why I had to leave.

———•———

THE CRACKS BEGAN APPEARING after John and Janaki's civil ceremony. Even though Dad was around, he was in a weakened state. After successfully keeping Ma away from their wedding without repercussions, Janaki knew Ma was fair game. She started needling Ma and kept her on the defensive. Even Fredrick Winslow Taylor, the American Efficiency Pioneer, would have stood aghast watching our efficiency expert at work. Ma did not confront the woman on a mission. The dam broke after Dad's passing, and the flood subsumed us as Janaki entered her element. Janaki's beautiful exterior hid a feisty, entitled woman used to getting her way. In reality, a shrew. A Katherine who needed taming, I suppose. However, John was just a john, not Petruchio.

While I mistakenly believed, John and Janaki were trailblazing heroes, out to crush customs and mores and leave their mark for others to follow, their crusade ultimately started and ended with themselves. Standing before Ma, ready to depart, I remembered my heartbroken Dad's Malayalam truism, after John's civil ceremony, and how he had foreseen the inevitable outcome.

———•———

MA PRESSED SOMETHING into my palm. Her *minnu-mala* (necklace with a gold cross) stared back at me. I had seen her jewelry disappear one by one to feed Mr. Primus and the household, but this one was her absolute last one. The cross, consisted of seven tiny spheres of gold—three across and four vertical, forming a *minnu* (cross) inlaid onto a thin gold banyan leaf. The banyan tree leaf symbolized protectiveness, and my parents protected us with every breath of their being. Our eyes locked in an embrace. How much I loved this woman. She insisted I take it, but how could I? She was practical as always and knew that the 20 rupees she had given me earlier would not last.

I thought of how the minnu-mala had adorned Ma and the story behind it. The history contained in the minnu is what I remembered from Ma's reminiscences—Ma's marriage to Dad. The preparations started with the bride's brother preparing the wedding necklace. Since Ma's only brother died a year earlier, Ma's older relative prepared the necklace. He extracted 21 gold-coated threads from the *manthrakodi* (the bride's silk wedding sari), entwined them three at a time to form seven strands (three and seven because it stood for indivisibility), and needled them through the eyelet of the minnu, creating a necklace. Then, he taught Dad how to tie an *Aan Kettu* (reef knot) with the seven strands. He placed the necklace in the folds of the manthrakodi. Dad stood behind Ma at the wedding and tied the silk strands with a reef knot, thus adorning Ma. He replaced the silk threads with a finely braided gold chain a few weeks later.

No way could I walk off with the minnu. I unclasped the necklace and removed the minnu. I placed it in her palm. The minnu would remind her of that day in the *madhuba* (altar) of the Mar Thoma Kochu Palli, all those years ago, when Dad had tied the knot so expertly. The tiny cross would remind her of the necklace she had given me, which I had promised to hold on to as long as possible. I held her in my arms one last time.

Like Dad, who left his home decades ago, I was departing mine to save it by not being a failure. As she placed her hand in mine and looked up, I could see her trepidation, the hopelessness, and the utter sadness in her forlorn eyes. I looked down, forever her errant child, as I imagined Dad watching over us sadly. I placed my hand over hers.

These hands had bathed, loved, nourished, fed, disciplined me with a rolled-up newspaper and the dreaded Abhayangam, and thrown the ball as we played cricket. She lifted my hands to her face and inhaled deeply. In turn, I took her hands and brought them to my face. I detected the faint fragrance of cilantro leaves. It would probably be a long time before I tasted her meals.

The aftermath of Dad's death stunned us senseless. My father's house needed saving. That's when I discovered the mansions he built for me. I was the last one standing, a seventeen-year-old nobody, young and foolish, but willing to try my best.

———————— ◉ ————————

AFTER HIGH SCHOOL, Dad left home for Madras, 400 miles away, and started a clerical job. He was the first in his family to leave Kerala. Grandpa was ready for Dad to marry a Brethren girl and had the one in mind. Dad cast custom aside and let his father know the girl he had in mind—Rachel, a Mar Thoma Christian and the youngest sister of his classmate. He would marry her and no one else, and there would not be a dowry—another custom he broke.

That was my 'ahead-of-his-times' Dad in the 1930s, going against his father's wishes and marrying for love. He questioned authority his entire life. Although he did not see eye to eye with his Brethren relatives, he loved them to a fault. Starting from his first job in Madras, Dad helped them beyond his means. He helped his family fight poverty, and in the process, showed them how to take charge of their lives rather than relying on the afterlife, enter modernity, stop denying science, and embrace the truth.

Dad and Ma made sure their families and many others survived. He found mixed success in teaching them other goals he had in mind: to care for others who were not of their own kind, to embrace science-based beliefs, and to accept modernity. These goals became victims of the fallacy of circularity, like a dog chasing its tail. Why would his Brethren relatives do anything to better themselves when Dad was around to enable them to do what they did best—continue to believe and behave like a cult, pray at every turn, and procreate merrily? He poked fun at them as they seethed within, which only made things worse. I, too, loved them, but later on, I drew a line when I learned the extent of their righteous hypocrisy.

Dad and Ma were a well-synchronized team for 28 years, enduring all their self-induced hardships together. Without Ma's help, Dad could not have served all those youngsters who came to our door. She cared for them like her own children; they stayed for months and months, and she made sure none of us went to bed hungry. I can only imagine the countless meals my parents missed and the jewelry she pawned away in this effort. They were simpatico teammates.

⟶ ◉ ⟵

IN 2004, I VISITED an elderly cousin who was dying, the last patriarch of Dad's household, and a Brethren lay preacher who had grown up with Dad and was the second child to finish high school in Dad's village. My memoir, a tribute to my parents, had been brewing in my mind for a long time, presenting a once-in-a-lifetime opportunity. I was sure the cousin remembered their lives (Dad's and his) together as youngsters. I wanted to know if he remembered any *kathas* (anecdotes) from their childhood. He took umbrage at my requests and smelled an ulterior motive. Whatever he thought never crossed my mind, although I knew Cruella was his mother.

One of those days, after I made such a request, he looked at me unflinchingly and told me in perfect English that Dad was a good man and, unlike him, I was a wicked fellow. The amusing thing was that he had timed it so that no one else was in the room when he insulted me. Even near death, my cousin made sure of deniability. At first, I thought he was joking, but I soon realized he couldn't be joking in his condition. For sure, Dad did not need his endorsement. Dad futilely tried to get him to come to Bombay after he matriculated. Yet, the cousin chose to remain in his hometown, pray, evangelize, and procreate without a thought, while Dad carried most of the water for him. Who knows, maybe he even had a hand in lopping me off from the photo of Grandpa and me. All the English he learned was a waste—to have used it only to shock and flail me, his benefactor's son, while he lay on his deathbed.

On Sunday, I attended the Brethren meeting feeling dispirited after my encounter with my cousin. The constant drumbeat at all their Brethren gatherings, including weddings, was their self-proclaimed superiority of being 'the chosen.' There was enough discrimination without saddling a loving God with mean-spiritedness, choosing one group over another. During the sacraments, my relatives performed a pre-choreographed end run on me by passing the bread around me and avoiding me. I no longer felt like keeping up appearances. I envisioned Dad turning in his grave, shocked and surprised by my shunning. Stunned by my exclusion, I grabbed the wine as it passed by me and took a gleeful sip. I was sure that if Dad were in my place, they would have shunned him, too. I now understand why Dad cast his lot with the Marthomites.

It was sad to see their mostly subservient wives obey their spouses, even though they were the significant breadwinners—the RNs and the professionals. Their men did what they did best–came home from their factory jobs, behaved like royalty, and lifted their fingers only to turn the pages of the Word of God. With their penchant for quoting scripture and flaunting godliness, many of their children held extreme right wing, so-called conservative views, one up on their parents.

'Dad, was there a point?'

Dad answered without hesitation, 'Yes, *moné* [son], change takes time, and sometimes you must reach the bend in the road before you realize it's a dead end.' Dead End, indeed.

———◉———

CHAPTER 13 PICTURE: Dad and best friend (Ma's brother).

Dad and uncle were schoolmates. Dad cut a swell and dapper figure. It is how he dressed daily for the office until the accident. My uncle was a famous tailor for the Raj. His specialty was Western clothes. He died a year before Ma's marriage to Dad.

———◉———

———◉———

Chapter 14: Leaving Home

My plan to leave quietly went awry when Ma sobbed, and Janaki shot out of her room holding the baby, her eyes crossed in query.

"Where the hell are you going with all this?" she shouted, pointing to my knapsack.

She continued haughtily, "I knew something was up. I don't understand the drama. You want all the neighbors to know?"

My hushed conversation with Ma into the wee hours was none of Janaki's concern.

"So what, anything goes after what you and your parents did?" I broke my resolve not to speak if Janaki made a scene.

"You can't do anything without your mother, can you? Doing nothing to help, eating like a pig. If not for us, you both would be at the railway station eating *channa* [roasted chickpeas]." What she meant was we would be panhandling.

My brother broke in at the tail end.

"That's right, Janaki is right. You think this is a waiting room where people hang around doing nothing?"

Samson was in great supportive form. If it were a game of marbles between the two, he had lost his last one. Of course, he meant the waiting rooms at the train stations, which were always a big part of India. Oh, brother, where were you when the train was at the station? Besides, Janaki is right about being on the streets; it would be you two if Ma kept Dad's pension. No one advised Ma, not even Uncle George. Of course, I did not say anything, but I began to understand Dad's pithy Malayalam truism to Joseph after the civil marriage.

"Look, things are not the same after Dad died. We grieve for him. We have a baby to look after, and she needs all our attention now," replied John, in salvage mode. He wanted to maintain his position as the son, brother, and respectable physician—a doctor who cared for his fledgling family, his mother, and his siblings. My leaving home would trigger talk among the neighbors, and John did not want to be the one who drove me out. It was ironic, since he was the one who enabled the acrimony. Did they not realize I needed help? I threw caution to the wind after the two-pronged attack and voiced my feelings. Ma's lips quivered in prayer.

"I need peace and solitude to prepare for my exams, not a constant battle. Dad's pension was Ma's alone, and you both say we would be on the street? How recklessly you gave the entire pension away to the Nayyar brothers. They even chauffeured you and Ma to Dad's office to take off with it. They did not even allow you to smell or feel those notes. Not even a receipt. What a bloody joke."

My 'not forgetting' part took over. I reminded John how I endured his bullying and how I forgave and tried to forget. I reminded him of the 'Wills cigarette incident,' which earned him my final distrust. The two stood agape in silence as they took it all in.

I searched for articles about bullying within families; there were only a few until recently. My siblings made a classic three-pronged attack. The promise of acceptance was all it took to pull it off, and they did. First, they softened me with the name-calling and constant put-downs, which hurt my psyche and short-circuited my self-esteem. They controlled me by ordering me to run errands. The killer age gap did the rest—we had nothing in common. It is not something they planned. Siblings are usually allies. For a usurper like me, by depriving them by just being, I was not. I was ten years late for the party. My parents, whom I allied with, were my safety net.

Getting educated did not solely mean you could read and write. Dad took a high school education to the next level and beyond through relentless self-learning and reading, civic-mindedness, and a passion for learning and writing about politics, as well as helping others. He grasped the allegorical nature of scriptures and our place in them. He understood why one should never let religion kneecap you. Bigotry and intolerance of others slowed everyone down, including the perpetrators. Nobel laureate Rabindranath Tagore said it best in the poem 'Let My Country Awake,' in his epic collection of poems called Gitanjali or Song Offerings, written in Bengali in 1910, that he translated to English (circa 1912):

Where the mind is without fear and the head is held high;

Where knowledge is free;

Where the world has not been broken up into fragments by narrow domestic walls;

Where words come out from the depth of truth;

Where tireless striving stretches its arms toward perfection;

Where the clear stream of reason has not lost its way into the dreary desert sand of dead habit;

Where the mind is led forward by thee into ever-widening thought and action

Into that heaven of freedom, my father,

LET MY COUNTRY AWAKE!"

Dad and Ma woke me to the world I would live in. John allowed his in-laws to practice their hate in our house. Janaki's education proved inconsequential, and it was impossible to erase what her parents had meticulously engraved in her pliable mind. In addition, she had a sense of entitlement about herself—it was her way or eating channa on the roadside. The Shoreys unwrapped a timeless, well-preserved, shiny Brahmanical cudgel for all our neighbors to see on Dad's veranda—consecrated ground where my revered cricket stumps stood in testimony to the hate. The cudgel I refer to is the closed-minded bigotry they unwrapped in the house where they sought safety. A Vedic time warp distorted the three. To top it all, it happened in my father's house in a free and secular India.

⎯⎯◉⎯⎯

MY STUMPS AND I HAD come a long way together. They watched Ma and me play cricket when I was off from school. They guarded me when I studied into the night, and they kept a close eye on Dad when he paced the veranda like a madman with the loan shark nipping at his heels. Then it hit me. The smudged stumps were crying for help. They were all but obliterated after the Brahmins left them choking from the kerosene-fueled smoke of their cooking. It would be unthinkable to leave them as witnesses to their desecration, and I had to erase their very existence forever. It was justifiable euthanasia. I dropped my knapsack, retrieved my penknife, and proceeded toward them. My mouth was dry; I took each deliberate step toward my dear wickets. Without saying a word, I scraped the traces of the stumps and bails with the penknife. Janaki and John thought I had gone plumb crazy. The rasping sound—metal scraping distemper—caused my face to flush. As tears rolled down my cheeks, I remembered times like these when I watched Otta Kaiyan getting beaten. When I had obliterated the last remnants of the wickets with the dull blade, I expressed my final sentiments on what I had accomplished.

"There, I have done it, Ma," I continued through tears. "I have scraped my hallowed wickets and recovered their Ashes. If I could, I would have removed each stone slab from the veranda."

Nanda, Raj, and Bhaskar waited at the turnstile, ready to accompany me to Dadar. Thankfully, they could only hear snippets of the pair talking with Ma and me.

"My precious son, remember how Dad and the two of us faced those dark days. We can do the same together, and I'm sure those cricket stumps suffered with you."

"Ma, it's not about me and cricket. It's about us, Dad, you, and me—even them."

"My son, what should I have done? Do you remember what Yohanan told us that night? He promised to protect us, and I still believe him. He let his wife meddle away," she paused and took a deep breath. "I don't want you to leave because he will come to his senses. Yohanan, can I ever trust you to do right by Dad? Janaki thinks there is room here only for the three of you. Gandhi told the British that there was room for everyone if no one took advantage of others. To tell you the truth, I have... "

I interrupted her instantly. In addition to the kitchen jujitsu Ma performed for Janaki in her eternal quest to save kerosene, I remember the verbal humiliation she piled on Ma. I felt this was a rare moment of elucidation when her one question to John dangled unanswered. Lucid and clear, Ma was like the one who stood me up in front of her and explained the evils of smoking. John and Janaki appeared taken aback at Ma's newfound strength. For an uncommon woman like Ma, it was always a matter of truth versus power. I knew her firsthand, and she provided the opening I needed.

"Ma, I can't wait any longer for them to change. They ignored Dad's cries for help. See what they've accomplished in just a few months. Trying to get rid of us after taking your pension is what it's about. Ma, do you know what happened to Hindu widows in the past? They called it Sati, or self-immolation. Nowadays, they send them off to the widow farms. Widows are useless, and Janaki comes from that mindset. Remember that Dad's pension paid those crooks.

Had Uncle George or someone like him advised you or helped you guard the pension, I would not be standing here ready to leave. I know your heart and your belief in John."

We had our conversation as if they were not around. When we both stopped, it was gunshot quiet, as if in its wake, with smoke curling out menacingly, like a reptile. I looked around. Happenstance, I spotted my drawing board and tee behind the door, which I had forgotten in my state of mind. I retrieved the items and walked toward my knapsack. The two were silent, and Ma stood by as if it were another funeral.

I then turned to Janaki, "I don't see why you hate Ma so much. You knew we had a special bond with her."

I faced John one last time. "Yohanan—don't stand there so dumbfounded. You are not clueless, with all that wit and brilliance, are you? When I leave, you have only Ma to care for."

For once, although Janaki narrowed her eyes to reptilian slits ready to strike me she did not say a word because she knew I was right. Who knew what was in store for me? Perhaps she knew she had won a battle when, in reality, she had won the war. Maybe it was not my imagination when I saw her lips twisting with glee, provoking a fight so she would see my dreams blow up in my face. I paused at the look of schadenfreude she gave me, knowing she would soon have Ma all to herself.

I broke her smugness with a warning, "My friends will check on Ma."

I heaved up my knapsack, ready to leave. My friends, solemn-faced, hurried to our front door and picked up the rest of my belongings. I bent over the baby and pecked her forehead. For the last few months, she kept me coming back home. I hugged Ma one last time.

We crossed the railway lines silently and walked the concrete gangplank over the sewage drain. I took one last look at my father's house and waved goodbye. Ma was waving and beckoning me at the same time. I felt my Ma's necklace and ten-rupee notes deep in my trouser pocket. I felt reassured and happy to have someone who cared enough about me.

I remembered a Tamil lullaby that Ma sang to me that she had learned during her days in Madurai. She often sang it before my naps, and I thought they were about chickens and hens. I later learned she sang this song whenever she felt homesick in Madurai and thought of her mother. Ma's Tamil lullaby, *Aasai mugam marandhu poche, idhai yaaridam solven adi thozhi …?* (I have forgotten that lovely face, who shall I share this grief with, friend…?) had stayed with me through all those years. She let me think she was singing about hens. I hardly knew what the words meant then. I later learned the meaning of the song from Ma.

Ma may have misled me, or maybe I misheard the word *'thozi'* (a friend in Tamil) and took it for *'khozi'* (hen in Malayalam).' The song harkened back to her days in Tamil-speaking Madurai, where she trained as a nurse's assistant for a few years as a young teen. It had nothing to do with chickens and eggs! I figured the lullaby was for me during those hunger-filled days when I could not even remember how an egg tasted. It made more sense when I learned the meaning of the song. Even though Ma was preoccupied with our lot, she pined for her mother as she sang for me. Ma, the youngest, remembered how her widowed mother struggled with her brood of four, a boy and three girls. She never understood until much later why her mother lit the firewood she had made her fetch every evening, even though there was nothing to cook many evenings.

Subramania Bharati, a renowned Tamil writer, poet, Carnatic music composer, and Indian independence activist, wrote the song about his mother in the early 1900s. She died when Bharati was five. He was distraught as he left home for good in his mid-teens and realized that he had lost the only photo Bharati had of her to remember her by. He wrote the poem, which later became his well-known song, when he, or others after him, set it to music.

I was already missing Ma when I waved to her one last time as I turned my back on B1 (2). Even though, like Bharathiar (the yar sound in Tamil, after a name, is a mark of respect), I did not possess a photo of Ma. I was hoping the teenager Bharati's anguish over trying to remember his mother's face would not befall me. Could it happen to me? How could I ever forget Ma's kind and gentle face? I could never forget, even if I wanted to, the faint L-shaped scar on her forehead, a cause of headaches all her life after she fell and hit her head on a sharp piece of rock as a child.

My spine stiffened as those thoughts made me feel more committed. Ma's love, the lengths she went to care for me, and the final act of giving me her worldly possessions instilled in me a sense of resolve not to let her down and to stay focused on attaining my goals. Such thoughts bounced around like a gymnast's tumbling routine on the road to Dadar. After all these years, I still see my mother's face in all its detail and remember her as if it were yesterday. It would be unthinkable to forget a saint I lived with.

After Ma's face melted away, others came into view—those of my faithful friends walking ahead of me, and those who could not come. I was the prodigal returning home to where a building stood, whose windows beckoned me to be curious about the world around me, back to Main Road and Otta Kaiyan.

Since I was nine, I had left them collectively idling in my memory when taking care of Dad became our mission. Would my decision to escape back to a tenement in Dadar, be better the second time around?

Then, the image appeared of two happy nine-year-olds floating by, looking for a stolen diamond. That was eight years ago when Kamala and I crept together, searching for Chinka and Vijaya. We went to more nooks and crannies than ever before that last time. I whispered to Kamala that I would soon be gone. Our eyes got so close that I could feel her lashes fluttering against mine. Then I saw the golden downy fuzz on her face zooming out of focus as I finished whispering. She consoled me then and told me that as we lay on the shiny quartz floor waiting for the robbers, we would both be in Ruia College together soon. She would be a year ahead of me and would look for me when I joined college. She promised to help me with my studies. We would meet in the canteen and hang out together, eating samosas and drinking *Vimtos* and *Mangolas*. Then, we would study together and she would even help me. I had to find my partner in crime, who had so occupied my thoughts at the time.

'Mathew, did she mean that much?'

"Maybe," I said under my breath.

Several teardrops splattered on my sandals, mid-stride. I could not even imagine going to Sawant's tenement and asking for her. It would be a severe breach of Indian customs and mores. Even innocent friendships between the youth of the same caste or religion, let alone different castes or religions, could land them and their parents in trouble. The kind of repression and shame that the baggage of caste, creed, color, you name it, could bring to bear could result in sorrow all around. This kind of thinking and behavior has been pervasive and constant. Almost all Indian marriages were 'managed' and 'arranged,' negotiated between the parents based on the dowry size and not much else. The results of my brother's experiment were sinking in. I had to find Kamala at Ruia College. I would keep it low-key and not behave like John's lovelorn Mario. If I were to run into her, that would be fine. I resolved to study for an hour or so at the Ruia library on random evenings. She attended King George High School, a stone's throw away from Ruia College, which had a significant influence on my unconventional thinking. Since most of the smarter college-bound kids from King George ended up in Ruia's, there was a chance I would get lucky, assuming

Sawant sent her to college, which would be a first in the family. As I increased my pace to catch up with my friends, so did my heartbeat. I realized no matter what, I was getting closer to my old friends with every step. I set aside my thoughts, hurried to where my partners lived, and took a deep breath.

The fleeting image that shimmered ahead was of Kamala eight years later, in the full bloom of her youth. She clutched her books, prim and proper as ever, and hurried to college. Then the other two, Chinka and Vijaya appeared, rushing about with a purposeful glint in their eyes. Chinka, with a briefcase in hand, headed to his father's business, while Vijaya, in high school, rushed to the same high school as Kamala, wearing her white and blue uniform. The reality facing me looked daunting, despite all the resoluteness I had conjured up. Memories of my time in Dadar, cherished and forgettable, started flooding back. Walking into the unknown, my purpose in tatters, confidence shaken and fraught, I was now the laggard.

What is a homecoming without a home? Even so, I was getting back to where I belonged. You can take the boy out of the tenement, but it was proving impossible to take the tenement out of me.

———◉———

A NOTE FOUND IN DAD'S green notebook:

Ma, John, and the Nayyar brothers collected Dad's pension on February 18, 1966. After writing a check for Dad's final borrowings from his office mates (shown below), the brothers took off with the rest of the pension for the promised flat.

———◉———

Shri   A. K. Patwardhan   Rs 150.00
  „   J. D. Marolia   Rs. 30.00
  „   Bhaskar Dhादoo   Rs 150.00
  „   G. Naronha   Rs 200.00
  „   S. Madhavan   Rs 150.00
  „   R. J. Mchendale   Rs 30.00
  „   S. N. Rawool   Rs 70.00
  „   V. A. Pradhan   Rs 125.00
Miss Karande.   Rs 60.00
  „   Motkur.   Rs 40.00
                    Total   Rs 1006.06

Cheque Paid to the Marolia on 18/2/66 for Rs 1006.00 for payment to all

Chapter 15: Belonging

My friends stayed as we awaited Abdul Rafi at his building, which stood south of Sabita on the same street. With dusk fast approaching, I told my friends they could go home. They left me surrounded by my belongings as I watched my last ties with Wadala slip away.

Abdul arrived soon. Smiling, he quickly led me upstairs to meet Mrs. Karnik, with whom I would lodge for the next few months. Hastily, Abdul closed the door behind us at Mrs. Karnik's flat. He departed soon after introductions. I don't suppose he wanted to draw undue attention to himself. Mrs. Karnik seemed nice, much older than Ma, and a widow like Ma. What distinguished her was her mane of silky white hair. She was a high-caste Hindu, also known as CKP, like my friend Vijay, since their surnames were identical. As her eyes roamed around my belongings, what most intrigued her was my drawing board and tee.

She showed me my room and enquired about my exams, perking when I mentioned the IIT exam. I also informed her that I was a first-year architectural student at the College of Architecture and was studying for its exams. After asking me how far apart these exams were, she realized I was studying for two sets of difficult exams a month apart. She was a Montessori teacher, now retired; her husband, a retired school headmaster, had died ten years earlier. The room was Spartan and had a desk, a folding chair, and a *charpoy* (coir bed).

Mrs. Karnik said it was her *pooja* (prayer) room until recently, which explained the faint fragrance of *agarbathi* (incense stick). She informed me she had moved the small shrine, the pictures, and the floor-level stool to her bedroom, adding that she could start the day singing the aarti. I smiled knowingly and hoped she was not off-key like Janaki. I thanked her, enquired about the rent, and assured her I would start paying rent after finding work. Shrugging her shoulders, she indicated the rent was unimportant and said, "You don't have to worry about the rent just yet. Do all your exams well." I was pleased with how well Otta Kaiyan presented my situation. I had a rent amount in mind, remembering the many times Mr. Pestonji, the Parsi rent collector, showed up at 24, Sabita demanding 22 rupees for each month Dad was in arrears.

Back in my room, I was alone and scared. Bent over, head buried in my hands, the events of this heavily charged day thrust me into a void. Finally, I picked a textbook and turned its pages to escape the funk. I studied formulae and wrote them down, starting with the basics. I repeatedly recited the proof of their derivation, hoping the repetition alone would make some of it stick in my unsettled head.

A worried Mrs. Karnik poked her head out, and seeing that I was studying, she brought me strong chai, as Ma often did. That first night, Mrs. Karnik asked me to join her for supper, and while eating together, I told her not to worry so much about me. I returned to my room and continued the late-night nightly recital through the first weekend and into the week, completing the task by late Sunday evening.

I now had a stack of sheets. Mrs. Karnik found some twine for me, threaded it through the pencil holes I had made in the sheets, and we adorned the room with it. She now saw through my monotonous recitals, murmurs, and groans and felt reassured I had not gone bonkers. We had another simple meal, and after that, Mrs. Karnik scooped a large dollop of *shrikand,* a mouthwatering sweet and sour Maharashtrian yogurt dish, and served it with purees. To cool my brain and help my memory, she said. After completing the festooning, I realized we had turned my exam preparation into a celebratory event, a celebration of my future. With formulae all around, I felt I was drowning in them.

I attended only architecture-related lectures and did not attend the Science and Math lectures, as the IIT preparation took care of them. I spent my spare time in the college library and at the Ruia College Library for an hour. The original intent of finding Kamala at Ruia yielded nothing, although changing venues helped alleviate the monotony and improved my studies.

I tested my problem solving speed and accuracy by how fast I could recall the relevant formulae that applied to each problem. My memory often sputtered like Mr. Primus, and when I groaned, Mrs. Karnik showed up furrowed with worry. Finally, I sucked them all up and gave Mrs. Karnik a break.

Those humdrum days of plodding through tedious studying found me knee-deep in the quicksand of solipsism. I hummed Ma's lullaby and Dad's hymns to escape my useless self-examination and reveries. Bouts of self-pity led me to daydreaming, and I found myself in imaginary conversations with them, begging me to stay focused. The past was gone, and torturing myself would do nothing.

One evening, I found my festoons had vanished. I whipped around, looking for Mrs. Karnik. I found her in her favorite chair, reading a newspaper, as I skated to a stop. Newton's first law of inertia flashed through my mind after I regained my balance. A body at rest remains at rest, and a body in motion stays in motion unless acted on by an external force. Mrs. Karnik was at rest. Had I remained moving, I would have crashed into her. The friction between the floor, my sandals, and my willful decision to stop brought me to a screeching halt. Maybe all that Science and Math was getting to me.

"Hey, Mathew, are you looking for these?" Mrs. Karnik enquired with eyebrows raised. She moved the newspaper from my line of sight, and there they were—my festoons eyeing me.

"I was . . . I am Mrs. Karnik. Sorry, I'll tidy up my room and make sure they don't come loose again," I apologized.

"My dear boy, nothing of the sort happened. I removed them to copy them and help you as much as possible. Please sit down and let us start our daily exercise."

With that, she read aloud the most basic of basic equations.

"What is the equation of a straight line?"

"$y = mx + c$. Mrs. Karnik, you don't have to do this, please."

"What is m?"

"Please, Mrs. Karnik... it's the slope.."

"What is c?"

"The Intercept. Oh, Mrs. Karnik, please."

"On what axis?"

"Oh, x-axis, I think. *Maja Áieé* [my mother in Marathi], are you sure you want to do this?" I had inadvertently elevated her to my Ma because she reminded me of Ma taking charge.

"Wrong. It's the y-axis."

"Yes, Mrs. Karnik, you are right."

I clucked my tongue at my flippant mistake in answering the most basic equation. It looked like there was plenty of slogging ahead for me. I thought about it and remembered its diagram in my textbook. Visualizing and making a mental picture were the keys.

That said, I approached Mrs. Karnik, genuflected, and kneeled. My newfound mother cupped my head in her palms, gently raising it so we could look at each other. I knew the Montessori teacher had taken over, and in turn, I had found my surrogate Ma, ready to play cricket with me. It took a CKP like Mrs. Karnik to set me straight. How ironic that Dad had warned me about the dangers of not keeping an open mind!

"Yes, *aré beta* [son], we will do this daily as long as you want. I will write these down and restore your garlands."

I was speechless—she had just called me her son. I needed her support, a sense of belonging, and *mamta* (mother's love). I trusted her as I did my Ma. I went to my room, brought Ma's necklace, and gave it to her for safekeeping. I told her why Ma gave it to me, and the story of the missing cross. Deeply moved, she ensured its safety. She expressed her desire to meet my unusual mother, so I gave her my mother's address.

Money was becoming an issue as Ma's twenty bucks dwindled. Rent would soon be due. I had stretched the twenty quite a bit by eating little and drinking plenty of water and tea, which was getting untenable. I beat the pavement for days around my college and Ruia College areas, looking for a desk job or suitable part-time work, but I could not find any.

Finally, I sought Otta Kaiyan's help and left him a note in the stairwell, as he had told me to if I needed him. He informed me he had already talked to Sawant sahib about me, and Otta Kaiyan said he would soon arrange a meeting.

The great man summoned me to number 32, Sabita, after midnight the next day. Since I was a special case, Otta Kaiyan told me Sawant wanted to talk to me directly, not through his goons. Sawant, he said, wondered aloud why a college-going kid wanted a job, especially in his outfit.

I left Mrs. Karnik's flat for our meeting the next night after hearing the stores shuttering up. The dust and the din had finally settled on Main Road as I approached Sabita building. Some stray dogs lingered around, some even making eye contact with me, telling me I had overstayed my welcome. I moved in the shadows from one storefront to another, avoiding the tired store workers who were asleep on the sidewalk. I continued until I was opposite the entrance to Sabita building and waited there for a few minutes, scouting the area before darting across and climbing the dimly lit stairs. I hurried by Prema's, Sharad's, and Chinka's tenements. I wasn't sure if they were still living there. I paused at the bottom of the stairway to Sawant sahib's floor. I recalled a diminutive me, stationary in that stance, waiting for Vijaya to bring Kamala. I brushed away the thought. Perish the sentimentality.

Circumstances had chased me into the spider's lair, and I had now casually reduced it to a past luminescence. Here I was—perhaps the smartest of the lot, handicapped by fate—another goat in the chain—climbing into the unknown against all common sense.

I knocked on the door according to the code Otta Kaiyan gave me. I heard two latches slide before the door opened to a well-lit room with a candle flickering behind a man who stood aside to let me in. He was unmistakably the Sawant sahib I knew. His face had wrinkled; his Brylcreemed, jet-black, wavy hair showed a hint of henna, and his nose had become bulbous with creeping spider veins. His jowls narrowed down to a thick neck creased with talcum. Although I was taller, looking down at him, though less intimidating, was still scary. His lips widened into an all-knowing sneer as he beckoned me into his parlor. The mouth revealed opulence—gold teeth stained dark red from chewing tobacco-laced betel.

Not knowing what to do next, I introduced myself and struck out my hand. Seeing through the cabbage patch of my emerging mustache and my breaking voice, Sawant ignored my sweaty palm. I quickly recovered and folded my arms in a namasté position, which he brushed off impatiently. It was not going well. He was in the business of keeping people on edge and was already one-step ahead of me. He cracked his knuckles, seized my collar in a powerful grip, and pulled me down, his mouth close to me. The smell of alcohol suffused with talcum was nauseating. He dragged me towards a tiny table that held the candle, a water container, and a sharp knife. I trembled at the thought of what awaited me.

"I met you because of your father and Abdul. Your father was a brave and good man. I found a job for you. I need an SSC pass to count money for the Matka business. I need honest people. Start tomorrow night before the daily 'open' announcement. After counting the 'open,' and the previous day's 'close' takings. I will pay ten rupees daily. Call me Sawant sahib."

"OK, I will, Sawant sahib," I whispered.

"Loudly, you moron. I can't hear you."

"Yes, sir, I will," I repeated loudly.

With his left hand still choking me, he pulled me closer to the table, took hold of the knife, and exposed the blade to the flame for a few seconds. He dipped it in the glass of water, and as it sizzled, he took my arm and cut my skin with two quick slashes. The blood gushed out as the seconds ticked away, and it was all over before I could scream in pain. Unlike a blood oath with a pinprick and an intermingling of our blood, it was a blood bath.

"Not a word to anyone about my business or Abdul, *samjé* [understand]?"

"Yes, sir, Sawant sahib," I shouted so he could hear and not get back to his bloodthirsty ways.

"Here is the key to the room in Dadar Wadi building, and this other key is for the safe.

Here's a tenner for today," he said, thrusting the money and keys into my chest.

Shocked and temporarily immobilized, I held a hanky to the wound and followed up with a craven 'yes.' I did not quite understand the nature of the job—counting money for two hours every day. Above all, why trust me? Maybe he was doing me a favor out of respect for Otta Kaiyan and Dad. Why slice me up for a two-hour job? I guessed Sawant sahib enjoyed intimidation and had to keep me scared enough from spilling the beans.

"Listen, you take the money daily from the kitty and note it in the book."

He blew out the candle and turned off the light. The room went pitch-black, and he nodded towards the dark veranda, dismissing me. I was now a gang member like Sharad.

I staggered home to Mrs. Karnik, who opened the door and returned to her room without a word. The blood had dried by now, and I was sure she saw the gashes. She probably thought the skirmish I got into was no concern of hers.

I told her everything the following morning. I did the right thing by telling her, because I suspected she would have shown me the door if I had kept quiet. Shocked and sad, she listened with rapt concern.

She lent me her wholehearted support when she understood my predicament and helped me keep it all together. She winced at the red-crested X on my forearm and reacted, as Ma would have. I assured her I had not turned into a slippery banana peel and would prove to anyone who cared that this was simply a means to an end, and I was not about to waste my life.

She rushed out of the room and returned with medicines and cotton wool. As she cautiously cleaned my wounds with a cleanser, applied Mercurochrome, and dressed the cuts, she asked me why Sawant had to hurt me. She seemed to have the same doubts as I did. Did Otta Kaiyan not mention the temporary nature of the job, or is that how he had to sell it to Sawant?

A few days later, I paid her the rent and bought her a box of Karachi halva. I entrusted Mrs. Karnik with most of my money. I offered Abdul money, but he refused. From then on, I hid some in the stairwell area for him.

I tried hard to stay focused as I got busier with architecture classes, the Matka job, and the IIT entrance studies. Thoughts of Kamala and other matters, all time-consuming and pointless, gnawed at me and slowed me down. What would happen if we met?

Would we even recognize each other? Was she still the same? I would have to meet her to answer them, which seemed unlikely.

My world now revolved around Matka and exams, a world, devoid of friends, and family; where dreams whispered and croaked. I made great strides and recalled most of the formulae effortlessly, although applying them to solve problems was another story.

Despite Matka being illegal, I admired its well-oiled efficiency. My limited knowledge of its operation is as follows: An individual at Matka HQ in Worli selects three numbers (from 0 to 9) from a Matka (pot) at 9 pm. He noted the sequence and added the three numbers. The second digit of the sum was the day's 'open' number. This information went to all the hubs. Similarly, he determined and declared the 'close' for the day at midnight. The open and close, in sequence, became the two-digit number of the day.

Betting on 'open' or 'close' numbers, one at a time, was inexpensive and made little, whereas correctly guessing the two-digit number cost a lot and earned more. Small bettors, mainly mill workers, are the bread and butter of the operation and bet on the daily single and two-digit numbers. Big bettors, more affluent and far fewer, bet on combinations of the six numbers drawn from the pot. It cost a lot more and paid a tidy sum.

I went to my workroom in Dadar Wadi around 8 pm, and a tall stranger knocked on my door with receipts and cash from the previous day's 'close.' After the 'open' announcement at 9 pm, he brought the 'open' receipts and money and picked the last day's 'close' calculations, receipts, and cash. After completing the work on the 'open' receipts, I took my tenner, noted the transaction, placed the ledger and the money in the safe, and vamoosed. The tedious work required concentration. Calculators were nonexistent. Reconciling the totals, in each betting category, which I refer to as accounts, was another matter. I wrote these down in pencil, with one column for each account. I repeatedly added the money in the columns of each account until I got it right, often until I was blue in the face. The totals had to match twice before I proceeded to the next column. There was a bright side to the endless toil: the daily mental jujitsu helped speed up my academic problem solving.

It soon became apparent that if Sawant got more big punters in the bag, he could make much more. The small time millworkers would always be there for him because they were his loyal, addicted followers—addicted to his liquor and numbers game. Since it did not take a genius to figure this out, and as sharp as Sawant was, he could cultivate the big bettors and bring in more of them using his charm. The payouts would not cost him much since the odds of big wins were small. He had many listed by name. A few names seemed familiar, but I could not be sure. Although the welts on my forearm had healed, they reminded me of the oath I had taken to do my job, collect my daily tenner, and keep my nose clean and mouth shut. Although the tenner was a pittance compared to the money I handled each day, it made all the difference for me—between going to college and dropping out, between having one good meal a day and going hungry, between sleeping under a roof or none at all, and between living in relative safety or on the streets. One might wonder why I chose this sort of self-sought misery. Was it to make a point? Far from it, I decided to pick physical discomfort over constant mental abuse. Preparing for my exams at home required someone with time—someone with gumption, and an ability to compartmentalize. For Ma's sake, it's sad that I didn't have any of it, especially time.

The architecture classes were going well, and I had almost caught up to the months of missed classes. Upon hearing about my long absence, a second-year friend was shocked and offered help. Others in my class were equally sympathetic. The outing on Sunday before we rushed Dad to the hospital had been my last contact with my class, and I disappeared after that for a few months. Although all the attention affected me, I knew I had to do it on my own terms and at my own pace.

The final design problem involved creating a memorial for unity that significantly contributed to my final grade. My professor was a retired architect who had worked overseas and occasionally threw in French phrases, to impress, that only someone who had learned French in school, like me, would understand. He assigned the design problem due at the end of the year while I was still attending classes. He talked about designing a memorial for the *jawans* (junior infantrymen) who died during the Kashmir War (1947-1948), the Chinese incursion in 1962, and the ongoing skirmishes between Pakistan and India. He spoke about the India Gate, Arc de Triomphe, and similar memorials. He also discussed utilitarian structures, both large and small, and libraries with the unity theme in mind. I heard not the highfalutin monuments to unity but his 'in-between-the-lines' emphasis on simplicity of design.

Most of my classmates went way beyond what I thought the professor wanted. Besides, I was only trying to pass Design, not waste time I didn't have. Examining some of their designs, I felt that mine would not meet the standard. I envisioned my 'Monument to Unity' project as a place where people went to relax. It would be much bigger than the center garden at Five Gardens in Bombay, where we went as children. In the center was a large circular pavilion surrounded by a garden for the many visitors.

The pavilion and base, featuring Jabalpur marble veneer, stood majestically on a well-kept lawn. Seven cobbled paths—seven representing indivisibility—radiated from the pavilion, set like spokes of a *chakra* (wheel). The chakra was in recognition of the Mahatma, whose cotton-spinning wheel symbolized the independence struggle. It even graced our flag. My monument had to be lasting. It had to unify without overemphasis, evoking a genuine sense of unity. It would be alive! It would unite diverse people, regardless of caste, color, religion, or social status—all of which have historically divided us. Visitors could gather and congregate in unity, enjoying one another's company. It would have four freestanding, overhanging, quarter-circle-shaped rooftops spreading from the pavilion center, like the protective sepals of a flower. These would rest on a central pillar located on the foundation. Two diagonally opposite quarter circles, covered on top with light-colored tiles, protected it from the elements. The other diagonally opposite quarter circles would have roofing with Mughal-design filigree work. The filigree design of the roof filtered the light, creating delicate shadows on the pristine marble floor. The changing patterns emerging on the marble floor refreshed themselves dutifully with the seasonal changes of the sun's daily traverse. At night, the roving moon took over this duty.

The two-foot-high marble base had well-spaced stairs on opposite sides of the circular base. In addition, there were two inclined ramps, similar to the ramp bridge I was accustomed to walking daily to and from the big school, for older people, located diametrically opposite and equidistant from the stairs. I scaled the design on a standard drawing sheet with front and side elevations and sketched a freehand perspective or isometric view for clarity. Of course, I could not show the filigree details, let alone draw the shadows it created on the marble floor. I pinned it to my drawing board and left it there daily as I worked on it. I covered my sheet with newspaper, as did the others, so each other's designs did not inspire us. The instructor moved from student to student, providing comments about their designs, questioning each one, and writing in his black book. It was a study in patience waiting for him to show up. A halo of curious classmates gathered around them when the lecturer queried the better student. During these interludes, I stayed at my desk, using my time for other items on my agenda. I was by myself when the instructor came to review my work. He stared at my design, and I heard him gasp.

I thought he was ready to snap my head off—done with me.

Chapter 16: A Spark in the Embers

He curtly asked, "Is this your work?"

"Yes, sir, it is. I can improve it, sir," I replied somewhat defensively.

"*Au contraire*, no improvement needed," he dismissed, smiling. Now for the carving and the skewering, I told myself as I waited for him to finish his thought.

"You have captured unity refreshingly as a living, breathing symbol. The overhanging circular quarters are thoughtful, as is the use of natural light through the lattice. The whole design is captivatingly familiar and unfamiliar at the same time. I am sure you know what I mean. You can certainly improve it; perhaps consider exploring ways to reduce costs. Modify here and there, and perhaps draw symbolic trees and flowerbeds along the seven cobbled paths, featuring people and children—but it is up to you. You have four years left to do the frills."

'Please, sir, let me be. Please give me an honest evaluation. I can take whatever you want to say and do what it takes to get a passing grade, sir. However, please be sincere with your evaluation because I don't have time for it. Don't string me along, *s'il vous plaît, monsieur?*'

He must have heard me thinking. Sensing my disbelief, he said, "I know you lost your father, and why you were away all these months. My comments are sincere and not influenced by your great loss. I am glad I mentioned the design problem several months ago when you were still attending classes."

He lowered his voice conspiratorially as he looked around. He continued, "Of all the students in the class, you are the exception who took it to the next level and made it look simple, bold, and effortless. You listened well and read between my lines—finally, such a breath of fresh air. We need free thinkers like you—young, uninhibited, and doing their best. Keep it up. *Merci beaucoup.*"

He then made a few notes in his black book. After giving me such a euphoric high, he left the hall nodding his head, looked back at me approvingly, and headed out. I dashed out of the hall, cheeks flushed. I did not have a sea of fellow students to wade through to reach the corridor to gather my thoughts, since no one had gathered around us to view my design. I sped to the canteen for a cup of tea, bounding down the two flights of stairs two steps at a time. Then it struck me: my professor had handed me a passing grade, maybe something much better. I would make some final touches and submit it. He had mentioned the project early in the year, which had a great deal of truth. Through Dad's illness, I wrestled with the 'unity' theme of the design all those months, gradually at first, and then went all out. The idea of unity allured and mesmerized me. It was what our divided country and my home needed in spades. When it came out on paper, it did so in a torrent in a few hours. What leaped to mind after the last sip of tea and the final drag of my Charminar brand cigarette was this from the Rubáiyát of Omar Khayyám.

The Moving Finger writes; and, having writ,
Moves on: nor all thy Piety nor Wit
Shall lure it back to cancel half a Line,
Nor all thy Tears wash out a Word of it.

Whether the poem had any context or bearing on my design, the sage's searing words were highly relevant. I had penned my idea in detail on the drawing sheet at home a few days before we rushed Dad to the hospital. An unseen hand guided me when it all came down on paper. I bent over the drawing board on my veranda—shirtless on that hot, muggy day as the three o'clock sun bore down, baking my bare back. It was the most sustained creativity, fueled by a torrent of adrenaline that I had ever experienced. I cared not for my physical comfort as I finished the freehand design, approximating the dimensions I had in mind. I completed the most crucial par—transferring my ideas to paper before forgetting them. I bent down to examine my work, the sun still relentless, and for some reason, my eyes internalized every square inch of the drawing. I rolled it up to transpose it to my submission sheet and pinned a fresh sheet on the board. Later, as caring for Dad took precedence and became a full-time task, I stopped attending classes. I never saw the sheet again after my sister-in-law moved my desk and drawing board. Soon, her parents took over that part of the veranda for their separate kitchen.

What awaited me when I returned to the design hall surprised and exhilarated me. My friends had taken the liberty of admiring my work. No doubt, they had eavesdropped on the lecturer's comments. A classmate, Rohini, a quiet South Indian beauty whom I spotted on the first day of class, seemed unmoved by the commotion around my desk. Not so the three 'devian.' They giggled when I discovered them gaping at my design, and I made a gesture of swatting them away, likening them to the industrial-sized flies that buzzed around a vendor's open cart of *khajoor* (ripe dates). I knew the girls liked me because they gave me the "glad eye" as I sang a cappella for the class at the picnic, but I didn't make any moves. I was a pauper preoccupied with my work, filled with thoughts of finding Kamala one day, often thinking of Dad and Ma, Mrs. Karnik, and my godsend, Abdul. They were my world now. That evening, I returned to my mundane but busy existence, brimming. I told Mrs. Karnik about my accomplishment. I talked to her about the three beauties I had swatted away, but did not mention frosty Miss Rohini or my search for Kamala. I thought of the two as I lay reading in my room. I had an embarrassing zero to show for finding Kamala. As for Rohini, she was unaware of my existence.

The words of the professor's commendation made life with my fellow students more amusing. Even Rohini seemed to be thawing as she smiled when we passed. We blushed when our eyes met, and I felt she had heard about the professor's comments. Then, bumbling like an oaf, searching for anything to say, I would squeak in a dumb greeting like a 'good morning' as I stumbled past her. As I turned my head to watch her curves slide, she turned her head, too. Briefly, our eyes locked before they slid away in embarrassment. In contrast to the three 'devian' who craved attention—eliciting catcalls for their effort with their loud colors, swaying hips, and revealing midriffs—Rohini breezed on by, not worrying about the wake she left, remaining slippery and elusive as a Boson particle.

Rohini's acceptance of my existence was reward enough, and I floated on a feather. However, when I quieted my thumping heart and quelled my thoughts, I woke up to my circumstances and goals and resigned myself to being content, smiling at her when we.passed each other. Even though it may have been all for naught, I decided to preen myself daily; it felt good to know my classmates were noticing me.

A few of them sought my help with their studies in the ensuing weeks. Since science and math were a repeat, I was the resident expert. In the library, I helped them with their basics. Some of the girls in the class bravely approached me for help. I don't remember all their names now, except for Rohini, with whom I spoke for the first time. I enjoyed my interactions with her; it was all business and nothing more. After classes, I spent more and more time in the Ruia College library, finalizing my preparations for the architecture exams six weeks away.

Then it happened. I met Kamala. Our meeting took place as if it were pre-ordained and unfolded perfectly. All the tables in the library that evening seemed more or less occupied. A table in a far corner with only one occupant had more than the usual number of chairs left at odd angles. I approached the back of the bespectacled head occupying it, and with the best baritone I could muster, I asked her, "Hello, can I take one of your extra chairs?"

The invisible face was preoccupied with several open-faced books, and it seemed her visitors had departed. She looked up at me as her black-rimmed glasses dangled halfway on her nose. Her piercing glance warned me not to be 'eve teasing' her. Eve teasing is a Bombay term for catcalling at close range.

Assured there was no such threat, she replied, "Oh, sure, please do. We forgot."

Before turning her head back to her work, I playfully said, hoping for a response, "Erudite," after observing that her spectacles brightened her face rather than diminishing it in any way. She looked up again with a vacant stare.

That is when my heart skipped a beat, and everything around me went awhirl. The glasses had thrown me off. I regained my composure and tried to remember Kamala from eight years ago. It was all there: the wavy, blue-black hair, all prim and proper, her double layer of eyelashes, her dad's nose, and the no-nonsense look of a police officer on the beat. I could not believe my eyes. After all these years, could it be Kamala? After weeks of searching, had it come to this—could I be this lucky?

"Kamala—you?" I blurted.

I could almost hear the cellist tuning in recognition of this celestial encounter. With fists clenched tight and knuckles turned white, the damsel was no doubt losing patience with this rude 'son of an owl' as her eyes glowered at me. Before she could question my familiarity, I broke the ice.

"Kamala, it's me, Mathew, your fellow police inspector."

The fists relaxed, her knuckles turned off their lights, and all the blood drained from her face. Her eyes lit up as she regained her wits, and her lips widened into her classic smile, displaying her even, lily-white teeth. She gathered her belongings in one lightning swoop. She whispered sweetly, looking up at me, "Let us go, Mister Erudite," in a measured tone. I was surprised she seemed to know what the word meant.

Her gaze sized me up, examining me as if to exclaim, 'Oh my, you've become this tall?' She might as well have added, 'Not bad looking either!' as her eyes melded into mine. I stood by, dazed and dazzled, and closed my eyes to take it all in. It had all happened as a nine-year-old girl predicted.

I held my hand out, and she shied away, saying, "Not here, not inside the building."

She looked back, smiling as I followed her like a puppy. Holding her hand lightly, I guided her across the road by Ruia College. She snatched it right back as we stepped onto the curb and walked into the *maidan*. My head was still spinning; I did not hear what she said, answering all her questions in monosyllables. Finally, we found a green patch and laid all our belongings next to it as we sat cross-legged, facing each other. The maidan housed the timeless Dadar Union Sporting Club, past and future homes to some of India's great cricketers, such as Madhav Mantri, Sunil Gavaskar, and Dilip Vengsarkar, to name a few. Dusk was creeping in, and I could see that the vast maidan was almost empty, except for a few youngsters playing cricket and a few die-hard fans like us.

"You didn't answer a single question. Are you going to say anything at all?"

My spontaneous comeback came with my best smile, "Only this, I am speechless."

At this, she chuckled, "OK, let's play speechless."

We both leaned forward and stared each other down like children until I blinked first and closed my eyes. When I opened them, I saw she had closed her eyes, too. I studied her face in total silence. She had left her face pristine and fresh –not even a smidgen of makeup marred the landscape. With audacity from God knows where, I leaned forward to brush her forehead with my lips, and then thought the better of it.

Her eyes opened, startled to discover how close my face was to hers. Without a clue of what almost happened but for my loss of nerve, she said, "Now tell me everything, *priya.*"

I did not know her use of the Sanskrit word *priya* (dear)—was it out of habit or a term of endearment? Only time could tell. For me, though, with that one little word, which would forever associate her with our encounter, she vaulted over all those lost years and brought me to a crystal-clear moment. For some reason, what floated by me was my brother's rendering of 'Then You'll Remember Me,' Thaddeus's aria from The Bohemian Girl. His was a less classical, less stuffy version.

> *When other lips and other hearts*
> *Their tales of love shall tell,*
> *In language whose excess imparts*
> *The pow'r they feel so well,*
> *There may be perhaps in such a scene*
> *Some recollection be.*
> *Of days that have as happy been,*
> *And you'll remember me.*

Maybe the last line of the aria should have been, 'And I'll remember you, my priya!'

Our eyes were swimming with tears as I began a condensed version of my long story since leaving Sabita. She had one excellent quality I admire in anyone. She was a good listener, interrupting me only a few times with a few kindly clucks. I was curious to hear as much of her story as possible that night. Sensing this, she said when I finished, "Mathew, one day, I want the longer version of your grim fable."

Before she began her tale, Kamala informed me that her family looked up to us, even though we were not Hindus. Ah, yes, it was everywhere—the grip of religion. She remembered Dad's accident, and she knew Sawant sahib had visited Dad several times during his recovery.

She heard that my brother had gotten into medical college that same year, and my sister would soon follow him. My siblings inspired her, and she set her goals high as well. Now, she could look back at what she had done, being the first in her family to reach college. She would retake the Inter-Science exam, a prerequisite for admission to medical school. Her exams were only a few months away.

She continued, her eyes softening, "How long I wished I would meet you. I thought I had lost you forever, but look at you now. You are already in architecture, studying for IIT, walking out of your house, and sticking it to them. You have become a brave soul, after all. By the way, Mrs. Karnik was my sister's Montessori teacher and is a sweet person. I must warn you that Sawant sahib is a ruthless and unpredictable individual. My brothers and many neighborhood children work in the business. Now you. Oh, my dear, look what you've done. He will be furious if he finds out we are friends. He dealt harshly with my sister and sent her to our grandmother in the village for a year, right during the school year, for talking to a boy she liked. Can you imagine something like this in this day and age? He tolerates me because I fight him. I am his favorite. I ignore him, and he cannot stand it. He treats his wives like chattels. I have no intention of ending up like them or my sister. I feel so bad for them. I would rather kill myself."

I reached out for her hand, but she only looked at mine.

"No, Kamala, don't talk like that. It is our time, our beginning. We have to look to the future. This awakening is bigger than us. We will be dear friends forever. We will meet once a week or so until we finish our exams, and after that, we will meet, walk, talk, and laugh about all those lost years. It is better this way, so much sweeter—this hiatus when we wondered whether we would ever meet again. Here we are professionals almost, because I guarantee you will soon be in medical college, and I will come and see you wherever you are and write to you. I agree we have to be careful of Sawant sahib."

It sounded too lofty, even for me, a teenager who had seen life's harsher side too early. She called him Sawant sahib like the rest of us did in deference and fear, instead of father, dad, or *vadil* in Marathi, and I did not know what to make of it. Then she blew me away as I listened, spellbound, to the rest of the story.

"When we were young, I often knelt by the window watching the street. Some evenings, you repeatedly shouted the same few words in your language. I was only a few feet away, remember? Eventually, I understood. You had spotted your Dad. I remember his quick gait. More yelling followed, but different words, which I think meant he had seen you as well. Sure enough, your Dad waved back heartily. After you were gone, I missed the racket you made. I remember it as if it were yesterday. I always wondered why he carried a big book; none of the other fathers did. After the accident, he carried a *pishwi* [bag] hung across his shoulder, with a book inside, I am sure. He did love to read, right? Probably all the family took after him, too. Did you know he led me? I started reading, too. Your family inspired me more than all those families in our building. I was getting the hang of English as a subject in our school when I started with English books and never looked back. I read more than I did homework: Blyton, Crompton, and others like them. As I grew older, I loved Mrs. Henry Woods and Austen and still read Wodehouse. Books took my blinders away. I also read Hindi and Marathi storybooks. Oh, how I envied you and your love for your Dad. I never had to wait for Sawant sahib like that. All I had to do was look down Main Road. Usually, he stood on the street corner surrounded by his *chélas* [followers], half-drunk, half-pissed, with a lighted cigarette trailing his hand gestures. He looked up occasionally and saw me at the window, but never waved back when I waved. Perhaps it wasn't the tough-guy thing to do. I gave up waving and hit those storybooks with only one purpose—to leave Sabita as you did. Did you know I looked forward to playing with you? I made sure you were my mate. I loved it when we walked together hand in hand. I urged you on, knowing there was not even a teeny-weeny chance Chinka and Vijaya would ever hide in those places. Oh, Mathew, how sweet were those days!"

Thinking back, it was all too much—as I brushed away the tears, hers and mine. I suddenly realized I had lost track of time since I had to be in the Matka office in 15 minutes. I would have to emulate Milkha Singh, our very own Flying Sikh of the late 1950s, and run as he did in the 400m Olympic sprint, all the way. Nothing like a one-sided blood bath to goad you, I thought cynically.

As she bashfully rose, holding my outstretched arms, Kamala allowed contact only for the briefest moment. She snapped her arm like a steel tape measure, springing back into its shell, transforming into her prim and proper self. We arranged our next meeting, and then I was off and running. As I looked back, waving repeatedly, she did not wave nor show a hint of recognition, resuming her serious demeanor. I felt a nagging sense of doubt and dread. It all felt like an improbable dream. It had to do with Kamala calling her dad Sawant sahib. Others calling him Sawant sahib was okay, but the same salutation coming from her seemed odd. The winds of caution were blowing around me, and I feared the worst; our friendship would endanger her and me. Ever since I started working for the man she called a 'dude,' I learned more about his dark side, more than she could have known or imagined. We had to perform well enough on our exams to escape his yoke and chart our own destiny. That is, if we decided to build on an old friendship. It meant work ahead for us, especially me, with my endless temporizing and all the baggage we brought.

Our meetings became shorter and less frequent as our exams drew closer, although we still managed to meet once a week. At our second meeting, I informed Kamala of Mrs. Karnik's address. I call them meetings because that's all they were—short meetings, so innocent. At the same time, my tangled feelings made me question our relationship. For now, I miserably rationalized—just seeing her, talking to her, and feeling intimacy without being intimate—all taboo in the 60s was enough.

Mrs. Karnik noticed my extra sprucing and grooming at home before our meetings. She could barely hold it together as I preened myself and hummed the popular Hindi songs of the day.

"Who is the lucky girl? Tell me, which of the three is it?"

I smiled, held back, and told her she would have to wait until I was free from my exams. Her face took the shape of a question mark and became a distraction, especially when there was little to tell. Finally, I gave in before the first exams. One evening, I sat cross-legged on the floor in front of her in the living room, ready to talk. Her ears perked up because she knew I was about to share something with her. I stretched the suspense playfully, knowing her imagination had gotten the better of her.

"I don't quite know what you are thinking, but here's my plan," I told her as she leaned forward like a trusting confidante. I continued, "I want to tell you that I will not have a stand-alone circular quarters overlap at the center for my memorial to unity, as I said earlier. It is expensive to have them overlapping and semi-freestanding at the same time. I will have one trunk-like pillar supporting the quadrants. The quadrants, shaped like large banyan leaves, will originate from the top of the pillar. Around the pillar, I will depict the Asoka pillar symbol. Maybe not an Asoka pillar. Lions can be an intimidating sight for children. Little fellows matter too, when it comes to unity. What do you think about these changes?"

"I think it's perfect. The large leaf-like quadrants provide shade and resemble the protective banyan leaf on your mother's cross pendant. Children would enjoy seeing natural symbols rather than lions. You think of every detail, don't you?" she observed, playing me along and smiling.

"Why are you turning red like a *chukandar* [beetroot] when explaining your design? Tell me, which of the three girls is it?" she demanded, cracking up. I could not hoodwink her, and she was right. I blushed too easily.

"To answer your question, there is no lucky girl. There is only unlucky me. Honestly, Mrs. Karnik, it is not them. I imagine the world of two other girls, birds of different feathers, flying around.

"OK, let's start with the first one."

Rohini was the one who came to mind, possibly because I saw her daily. I told Mrs. Karnik about her. I told her about a girl who caught my eye on the first day of college. She was unassuming and elegant, with no makeup except for a hint of kohl around her eyes. I told her she was the kind of girl you would take home to meet your parents, though in my case, it was only Ma.

Then I ran by her a small anecdote I wanted to get off my chest, which I was ashamed of. My classmates had started goading a braggart classmate into pranking Rohini. I lacked maturity for not speaking up, even though I wasn't in on the prank. They dared him to waylay her in the corridor and ply her with romantic nonsense. On the chosen day, I accidentally stood close enough and could not help hearing the fellow's drivel. Thankfully, she surprised me. Taken aback for a second, she turned red. Pulling herself together, she pluckily dispatched the ruffian with a wilting glare and a sneer worthy of a Kathakali dancer. She serenely walked past him without even deigning a verbal retort.

Mrs. Karnik responded to my revelation and wondered aloud if my spirited heartthrob had a name, and I replied that it was Rohini. First, she told me I had a respectful attitude toward girls and told me never to forget that. She shook her head in disappointment and said to me that my focus was getting away from me. We laughed when she shook her finger like a thermometer, felt my forehead, and declared that I was burning hot with a heart affliction. Although the Fever, like the song, tortured me, she made light of it all. Impishly, she asked me about the second girl, and I told her she was still flying around, but I would now bare all about her too.

"OK, Mrs. Karnik, I won't play a guessing game with you, especially when you see I am still turning red like a neon light. It is Sawant sahib's daughter, the youngest one—the one I have known since I was this tall," I said, raising my hand a few feet, indicating my height when I was a youngster. I thought I had hit her head with a truncheon because her face lost all composure, and she made gurgling sounds that became a coughing fit. I ran and got some water, and she started babbling between sips of water and fits of coughing. She told me how bad Sawant was, how he would spit her out, just as he had done to many neighborhood kids, and as for his daughter, he would do the same to her, too.

"*Aré, baba, yé tho unka ijjat ka sawal ho jayega, ullu ka patta* [Hey kid, it will become a matter of honor for him, you son of an owl or fool]. He will think you are mocking him."

Anything but that. Every Hindi movie had some version of the worn-out cliché, and Mrs. Karnik thoughtlessly used it. I realized she was consciously using the oft-repeated phrase to jolt me into full awareness of what I was getting into.

"Do you know he is a Maratha like Shivaji Maharaj [Shivaji 1, 1630-1680, a renowned warrior and wise ruler of the vast Maratha Empire who fought the Mughals and the English]? They are from the *Ghats* [mountainous range stretching along the coastline from

Gujarat state to Kerala] and are truly the descendants of fearless Rajputs, as they claim. You are a proud Orthodox Christian from Kerala. With your 2000-year history, you do not take any nonsense, either. Where will it end? Like me, I know you are more spiritual than religious, but this is the real world, not something like Gandhi or Tilak's imaginary world. You are both so young, with long, useful lives ahead of you. Are you stupid or what?"

I had never seen her so agitated, and I no longer felt playful. I had never heard anyone utter the word 'stupid' in that manner as if she meant it. I had to calm her down first.

"Or what, OR WHAT? Listen to me without saying I am both stupid and the son of an owl. That hurts, Mrs. Karnik. It reminds me of a previous life after my father passed away. Kamala is sensible and tough. She is not one of those doe-eyed girls who listen to their fathers and follow their husbands. Besides, she will be a doctor like my sister. Kamala is part of the new India, Mrs. Karnik, and we will see how our friendship works out. She is like Sawant, not scared of anyone, and stands up to him like no one else. Their chemistry is different, too, and Kamala does not fear him. He is clay in her hands. That's what she told me. We fight for everything, so why not fight for something that matters? We played together as children, holding hands, and now that I have found her, she shies away from the slightest touch. However, she is beautiful and speechless beyond words. We need your blessings, not your scary predictions."

From her stoicism, I concluded that bringing her around would take some effort. However, Mrs. Karnik surprised me when she met me at the doorway the next day.

"*Mera ashirwad* [my blessing]."

"You are like the child I wish I had. Kamala does not let you get away with anything—that will benefit you both. No, you are anything but stupid. Perhaps a bit too idealistic?" she said, smiling, looking down shyly, and nodding. "Don't ruin your exams thinking about it, and tell her it is her *maushi's* [aunt's] advice to her as well. Don't eat out tonight because we will celebrate with purees and shrikand."

I embraced her as if she were Ma.

Although my design had gained new friends and Rohini's awareness of me, even finding Kamala by sheer luck would be for naught if I did not finish what I had set out to do the day I left home. The design evaluation and the subsequent kudos told me that my compass was pointing in the right direction, and there were many more steps ahead for me in the next few critical months.

I knew her 'wet blanket' approach was what I needed, and maybe Kamala and I should cool it for good. Although her Hindi movie reaction had stung like a well-hurled truism, I knew she was right.

Chapter 17: The Son Also Rises

Kamala agreed we should heed Mrs. Karnik's advice to slow down until after our exams. She even planned to visit her newfound aunt soon after completing her medical college applications, while I was busy with my exam preparations.

Our exams, Kamala's and mine, held around the end of March, went well. She was unsure how well she identified a few specimens in her Botany practicals. During my architecture exam days, I continued my Matka job and took some liberties in arriving at the totals to save time. Mrs. Karnik provided me with meals and packed lunches during those days.

A few weeks later, I learned I had passed my exams. I informed Mrs. Karnik and wrote to Ma that I had cleared my first hurdle. It invigorated me toward my IIT exams a month later. I had done them reasonably well, and now my fate was beyond my control. I realized Architecture and Rohini would be history if I passed the IIT exams. I shuddered at the thought of failing IIT. I felt caught in a classic catch-22. It may mean returning home a beaten dog, back to *déjà vu*.

After my exams, I decided not to return home to Wadala, contrary to what I had promised Ma, and continued working. Knowing we would have the rest of June and perhaps July for ourselves, we took in Bombay's highlights during the day. While sightseeing in the historic downtown area, we spent time at JN Petit Library and the Jehangir Art Gallery next door. After walking by Dad's office in Ballard Pier, we visited the iconic Rhythm House, where we heard samplings of the hottest English and some Hindi 45 vinyl records, passing ourselves off as potential customers. We went to Dad's accident site, walked to Versova Beach, and had a picnic that

Dad had missed almost nine years ago. On the beach, like children, we acted out our lives with our families and enacted games we played with Chinka and Vijaya. We visited Ma and Ankita a few times. We had plenty to laugh about, along with Vimtos and Mangolas, not to mention samosas, sugarcane juice, and *neera* (palm nectar). I shared many stories with her about the accident, my narrow escape, Dad's passing, its aftermath, life in Dadar and Wadala, and how it had all affected and defined me. Since she was an excellent listener, I felt utterly *bindaas* (carefree) confiding in her. Was this a way to let go, I wondered. Even with all that prim and proper stuff, Kamala was funny, loving, and warm. Like Hansel and Gretel, we were becoming kindred beings, preparing for the world.

"Priya," she confided one day, "Look, we are together now. I never thought I would meet you. We must let go of the past, stop pitying ourselves, and move forward. I am also sad and angry with everyone taking me for a loser and calling me the daughter of a gangster's mistress. Our circumstances are similar if you know what I mean."

One thing that stood out in all this back-and-forth was that Kamala had no clue about her father's friendship with Abdul Rafi, and I told her it would be best to keep it that way.

Maybe those halcyon days were not supposed to last when I got word from Otta Kaiyan that Sawant sahib had summoned me the next night. Mrs. Karnik tried to calm me after the news, and I couldn't keep it from Kamala the next day. I saw that she was upset, just like me, but unlike me, she stayed calm.

What now? Perhaps he found out about Kamala and me. Maybe the Matka accounts did not balance. I wrote a resignation letter, not leaving anything to chance. I said everything I wanted to say, including thanking Sawant and reminding him how error-free my accounting was night after night.

That night, I avoided the shadows of the storefronts; instead, I walked in the middle of the road, keeping a wary eye on my surroundings for any movement. As I walked toward certain death, with footpaths to my left and right splayed with sleeping bodies, the occasional stirring stopped me short. Even the dogs and bitches of the night had vanished. Perhaps he did not want any witnesses as his mob slit my throat and threw me by the railway tracks—another statistic, another unfortunate Bombay commuter—who fell off a crowded train and died. I had my wallet and student railway pass, knowing they would get rid of both. I wrote my name and a few details on a tiny piece of paper, hoping the railway investigator or the police would find it. Even so, I incanted that I had nothing to fear but fear itself. I reached Sawant sahib's front door and knocked using the code I had used during my previous visit. The door opened, and Sawant sahib's oldest son, his right-hand man, stood there, unsmiling. He was the same height and build as the person who knocked on my Matka office door every night. Was he my executioner?

Ravi returned to his chair, while I stood by. The door soon slid open, and Sawant sahib stepped in, drink in one hand and a lit cigarette in the other. The ashtray jumped when he banged the empty glass on the table. As he sat, he waved me to sit down, and I nearly missed the chair. Seated, I was eye-to-eye with him, only the desk separating us.

"You want a drink?" he asked as he finished pouring and wagged the bottle.

"No thank you, Sawant sahib." If this were a test, I would not fall for it.

"Ravi, how about, you?"

"No Sawant sahib."

Again, I noticed how formal he was with his father. His children were either too respectful or too scared, always calling him 'sir' or 'sahib.' I was sure Sawant wanted it that way. I don't think they ever talked to him directly as children.

Sawant missed laying the cigarette in the ashtray's indent several times before succeeding. He rolled up his sleeves. He had something on his mind. I was in for a history lesson while he talked about my parents and siblings. He spoke of how brave my Dad was and how my parents cared for my siblings and me and helped many others. He said he felt privileged to help me. It seemed that I got the job for my parents' good deeds. He could have easily avoided all this midnight drama if that's what he wanted to tell me.

Abruptly, his demeanor changed. His eyes narrowed as he warned, "I want the truth. Last month and even last week, why didn't you make checkmarks on your worksheets like you always do?"

Before answering his question, I thanked him and told him how diligent I had been. I hinted at what he should do to develop his big bettors as he impatiently looked on.

Then I answered his question and told him I was busy with my exams, had not rechecked the totals, and did what was honest—left them unchecked. I asked him if I had made any mistakes, to which he gave me a non-committal snort and replied that he didn't like Ravi having to do any accounting, let alone so many recounts.

"Looks like you didn't take any money from the kitty either. Maybe I'm paying you too much."

Maybe that's what caused him to haul me in.

I said I did not mean for Ravi to do my job. I was ready with the resignation letter and placed it next to the ashtray, and Sawant sahib tried to read the words as I straightened it out. I should have known he was illiterate, at least in English, because he passed it to Ravi, who read it aloud, translating as he read. Abruptly, he waved for him to stop.

"You can work for me forever. You've done a good job," Sawant said, thinking it would ease my fear of losing my job. He thrust a hundred-rupee note into my chest, probably for those missed days, demonstrating his innate fairness.

Upon his urging, Ravi continued to read.

After hearing about my impending departure, he turned red and waved for Ravi to stop. I suppose my departure was the last thing he expected to hear. Then, he addressed the elephant in the room most threateningly.

"You think you can just leave? After all the training?" he demanded.

I could not tell whether he was serious, toying with me, or just being his irascible self. 'Give me a break. What training are you talking about?' is what I felt like asking. 'What do you want from me, Sawant sahib? Do you want to know the answer to your question? Let's see. Do you think I want a permanent part-time job? Do you think I passed SSC, finished my first year of college, passed my first year of architecture, and took the IIT exam so I could be your accountant? Why didn't you want to know more about the big bettors?'

Although this was my second face-to-face meeting, he had pitched his tent in my head for months. For one irrational moment, I stiffened, thinking he had discerned my impudent thoughts. I had nothing to give him in this seeming negotiation. He had also ignored my ideas about the big bettors. I was tired of being whipped around by everyone. Enough. I had to evict him from my thoughts and stand up like Dad, who fought each setback with courage. I had to make clear I was leaving; there was no negotiation here. I broke the silence and called his bluff.

"I will have my farewell drink now, Sawant sahib."

I scrunched my eyes to narrow slits so I could duck as he launched his fist at me. I heard him laugh. Ravi laughed, too. I slit my eyes open at the sound of Sawant sahib pouring a drink for Ravi and me. Speechless by the fact that he may have blinked, I lifted the stainless steel tumbler, raised it, and took a nervous sip. I recoiled as I drank the rest. How could he drink this horse piss when he could afford the best booze from the liquor store next door? It tasted much worse than the first drink Dad gave me when I turned 13, a *chota* (tiny) peg of Black and White Scotch at Christmas lunch. I liked the buzz but threw up Ma's special lunch and swore I'd never do that again.

"I have more to say and do," he said.

"What!" I blurted.

Then he said the darnedest thing.

"What else, *beta* [son]? Is there anything important I should be aware of? Anything you would tell your father if you could?"

'What else do you want from me, Sawant sahib? I had nothing to go by as far as I could tell, but maybe calling me 'son' had something to do with all this middle-of-the-night intrigue. Was this a trap?' I took the bait.

I was feeling the buzz. "Yes, Sawant sahib. About someone, you have known all her life. My friend Kamala."

I was sure he would hit me this time and scrunched my eyes again.

He guffawed, "Your friend, since when?"

He took a large gulp, smacked his lips, cracked his knuckles, picked the cigarette from the ashtray, and took a long drag. The suspense dragged on as he blew smoke into my face without a thought.

'Sawant sahib, do you want to know the answer to your question? Let's see. We have known each other since we were seven. Do you have a problem with that?' I stiffened again; sure, he was reading my thoughts.

"Is that true, Kamala?" he bellowed.

The door slid open, and Kamala stood prim and proper as ever. Next to her was her mother. Both stepped into the room, and I smiled. Kamala did not answer but looked down with such a deep blush that it seemed painted on. I stood up respectfully for Kamala's mother and shamed the two into standing up. At that moment, I could see that Kamala had him twirling around her little finger, and she was right all along—he was clay in her potter's hands. I leaned forward, ready to hold her hand. She appeared taken aback, as her eyes widened like those of a Kathakali dancer, telling me, the potten—so far, so good, I have this. Don't you dare eff it up.

"Yes, Sawant sahib, it is true. We've been friends since we were little and want to remain friends. That's all we ask, promise," Kamala calmly replied, looking expectantly to see whether he would say something encouraging. Her dad relaxed somewhat. There was a flicker in his eyes before they drifted into nothingness.

Certainly, Kamala and her mother had some gumption. They kept it short and sweet. It caused Sawant sahib to let his guard down; his wife likely persuaded him to allow their daughter to tell her story.

However, he did not wait. After quaffing the rest of his drink, Sawant squashed the cigarette into the ashtray, held back his wife with a drunken wave, and told the rest of us to scram.

Still, with a buzz in my head and much nervous energy left in me, I sprinted home. I took the easy path, the middle of the empty road, and rushed to tell Mrs. Karnik everything and show her I was still alive.

A few days later, I learned I had passed my IIT exams. The scheduled interview was a week from then. As I walked through the main gate at Bombay IIT the next day, in total disbelief, making my trial visit, I was stunned to hear my father say, 'Yes, son, you kept your word and did well. Never forget Mrs. Karnik and my namesake, the other Otta Kaiyan. They are Rachel and I in spirit.'

Dad's foresight about jotting down lost time in learning a new discipline to experience played out 25 years later. I realized how right he was when I designed and helped build Oklahoma City's Mar

Thoma Church in 1990. It still stands today on a two-and-a-half-acre plot. However, the church-building experience, marked by internal conflicts—such as the rejection of a jungle gym for the children and a bereaved father's withdrawal of the steeple funds amid bitter infighting—left me disillusioned. This, combined with the tragic circumstances surrounding the bereaved family's plight, who lost their 16-year-old in a car crash that spring, led me to leave organized religion. Based on that experience, I'm writing a short story book, 'Steeplechase and Other Stories.'

After a quick look around the IIT complex and the interview building, I rushed home to see Kamala. I had not heard from her or seen her in two days. I asked her to accompany me to IIT and then visit the lake adjacent to IIT. She had other plans. Perhaps she chose not to come, thinking it would be better to make her debut with me on the actual interview day. Was this choice hers alone? Then it hit me like a sledgehammer—was the meeting with Sawant sahib a mirage that night when he behaved and kept his fist to himself? Was he trying to lull me into a false sense of security? Did he order her not to go with me? Was it possible he would do something to scuttle our friendship? I looked for her as I passed Sabita. The questions kept coming as I went to my room. Mrs. Karnik was not there either. If there was ever a time I needed to see a friendly face, it was today. I fell into a fitful sleep from the sheer anxiety of it all.

A nudge in my side woke me up, and I was unprepared for what came next. Three beautiful faces came into focus. Kamala, Mrs. Karnik, and... Ma, really?

"About time you woke up. You have been making faces. What is the matter? Look who's here," Kamala said. A few seconds later, still kneeling beside me, she continued, "Surely, you haven't forgotten us?"

Still half asleep, I listened to Kamala and smiled weakly. My grimacing was perhaps due to a fitful dream, which had seemed too real.

"Ma, oh Ma," I exclaimed, embracing her when I realized that's where the two were, bringing Ma from Wadala.

My worries took a backseat as we celebrated the Moment. I was flush with tenners and decided to splurge on a well-deserved celebration—lunch at the posh Pritam Restaurant near Dadar TT. Kamala and I stepped out to talk while Ma and Mrs. Karnik conversed like best friends.

She had good news about her exam results. She received a first-class, but it was not good enough to gain admission to medical colleges in Bombay. I was confident she would get into one of the in-state ones and told her so. I asked her whether Sawant sahib would allow her to leave home. She told me she had to work on it and told me to stop reminding her about the sahib so we could celebrate with Ma and Mrs. Karnik.

We had a splendid North Indian meal. We enjoyed sampling and sharing—stuffed parathas, tandoori chicken, raita, pulao rice, and our favorite, *cholé-bhatura*. Kamala and I fed each other with a morsel of bhatura filled with cholé as Ma and Mrs. Karnik watched us—Ma opening and closing her mouth like a guppy as she often did, feeding me as a child. I ordered a special takeout for Abdul.

How could I ever forget my unsung hero?

Before Ma left with Mrs. Karnik for the bus stand, she took me aside and said, "*Moné* [son], I am so proud of you. Also Kamala. I ask God to guide you both in your studies and friendship."

I assured Ma we were good friends for now and that our studies came first. She clasped her hands around my waist and treated me like she always did, her errant child. Ma and Dad ensured my heart and mind were in the right place. After so many unsmiling years after the accident, Ma creased with a smile from ear to ear. She knew her last child was different from her other two. She and Dad knew I had to grow up in a hurry. She knew I could mop the floor with the smartest of the smart ones and not shy away from cleaning the toilet with the lowest of the lows. She basked in the gentle gleam of satisfaction of a well-done job, with love, patience, and reason.

Above all, she knew I would keep my promise about Kamala and me doing the right thing, taking it all in stride, staying good friends, and, first and foremost, putting our minds to doing well in our academics. The rest of it would follow in time. We could still dream big and walk the walk, hand in hand, as we used to when searching for the Kohinoor. We could even tilt our heads toward the sky and watch the moon follow us.

I was back at the IIT complex a week later, again alone. I saw Kamala's point of view in sending me off solo. She did not want to be a distraction. She wanted me to be one with Dad during the final stadium lap of my marathon.

That night at the house, Sawant was non-committal. Mrs. Karnik's warning was apt. Like a leopard stuck with its spots, Sawant could not change. Who would prevail, Sawant sahib or us? Kamala and I were two idealistic doppelgangers. What would her imperious father do, even though she had him under her spell? Being a Hindu with all its customs, how could the father overcome his loss of self-esteem when she turned the tables on him?

The scar on my forearm was a firsthand reminder and a warning I should never veer into his lane. Of course, Ma would swear by Sawant sahib. After all, he ensured that all the residents of Sabita received their daily water supply. He visited Dad several times after the accident, and I was among the few who knew how he cared for Otta Kaiyan in his own way.

Enough of this second-guessing, I thought. It was ruining perhaps the biggest day of my life. Once again, like Dad, I had to be optimistic even while facing a faceless phantom with hundreds of questions without answers.

'Son, remember what you accomplished. You cleared two major exams and became one of the few from all over India who passed the most significant one. I know how hard you worked and the resolve you showed. Set aside your worries and enjoy.'

'Dad, I visited your mansions and found my answers, although I did not know how returning to my roots would turn out. It was doing or dying—a lesson I took from the pages of your life. Dad, if I may talk cricket, I recognized the googly, my bugaboo, as I faced that last ball. I dithered between playing it safe and taking a chance. For one crazy moment, I cast caution aside and hit the ball before it bounced and tricked me with its misdirection. I lofted it into the fading sun and scorched it into the clock tower like C.K. Nayudu's sixer! I left it all on the field like CK.'

CK was India's first journeyman cricketer, a subedar in the Army, her first test captain, and one of Dad's favorites.

'Dad, your good deeds, yours and Ma's, affected Sawant too, to the point that he kept me employed and safe when I cried for help during those dark days when I had no one to turn to. What more could I ask?'

With my head held high and chest thrust out like a strutting sage grouse making his move, I entered the IIT complex for my acceptance interview in the summer of 1966. I knew exactly where to go because I had rehearsed it a week earlier. My efforts were finally seeing daylight. I had dared to imagine, as Dad had taught me. How beautiful is that! Was that not the whole point?

Calm ensconced me as Ma would with her arms around me. With my Dad leading the way, we marched onto that sceptered island of possibilities. Everyone in my small world looked on: Ma, Kamala, Otta Kaiyan, Mrs. Karnik, and even Sawant sahib—while Dad read aloud the note I hastily scribbled at the funeral. I had placed it in Dad's shirt pocket when we parted that last time: My Dearest Dad, I will be a good son to you.

About the Author

Mathew Daniel, a retired Aerospace Engineer in the US, transitioned from four decades in engineering in 2015 to writing about his formative years in Bombay.

With a passion for reading and storytelling and an eye for detail in 'My Father's House,' I bring to life my eventful childhood and a family's testament to resilience in the face of loss. It explores the unspoken family bond forged by fate and tempered by adversity.

About the Publisher

Mathew Daniel, Publisher, Oklahoma City, USA

I am publishing *My Father's House* through D2D Publishing.

My book is about my formative years in the bustling Bombay of the 1950s. Growing up in a one-room, third-floor corner tenement, the windows overlooking the busy street showed me the lives outside, imitating our own, the quiet confidence, like a silent river, running through the struggles and joys of daily living. I explore the tragedies that hit us hard and often, and how we faced them head-on and tried to survive.

Steeplechase and Other Stories, my second book published in 2025, is a collection of short stories. Among the 15 stories, one features a tale about my six-year-old granddaughter on her first day of kindergarten, when she gave me a teaching moment, and another story about a church I helped build, which ultimately lacked a steeple. A third story is about the Indian side of a friendship between two youngsters, one from India and the other from America, in the mid-1960s. They eventually renewed their friendship three decades later in 1995 in the aftermath of the Oklahoma City bombing.

Simpli Ma's Story, soon to be published in 2026 is biographically based - stories, vignettes mainly about my uncommon Ma, who, with her simple, common-sense, often humorous ways, pulled us through some hectic and difficult times.

My Father's House and Beyond is a follow-up book to My Father's House, about a friendship in 1960s Bombay, renewed in Oklahoma City in the 1990s during a turbulent time. The novel is centered around the time of the 1995 Murrah Building attack, when a friend at work lost someone dear to him in the incident.

Note: Mathew Daniel's Website: My site, Emdanielbooks.com, and my fourth book, Beyond My Father's House (BMFH), are both ready for simultaneous publication by the first or second week of June 2026.

The 'e' in the website name stands for *Elempilakal*, my Dad's house name in Tranvancore, similar to Simpli Ma's house name, Vadakanthotathu. It's a tradition seldom used anymore.

www.ingramcontent.com/pod-product-compliance
Lightning Source LLC
Chambersburg PA
CBHW031453160726
47994CB00005B/2005